WHITE COAT, WHITE CANE

WHITE COAT, WHITE CANE

*David Hartman, M.D.
and Bernard Asbell*

ЧªP

A Playboy Press Book

FIRST EDITION

Playboy and Rabbit Head design are trademarks of Playboy, 919 North Michigan Avenue, Chicago, Illinois 60611 (U.S.A.), reg. U.S. Pat., marca registrada, marque déposée.

Trade distribution by Simon and Schuster
A Division of Gulf + Western Corporation
New York, New York 10020

Designed by Tere LoPrete

B
Hartman

Library of Congress Cataloging in Publication Data

Hartman, David, 1949-
    White coat, white cane.

    1. Hartman, David, 1949-   2. Psychiatrists—Pennsylvania—Biography. 3. Blind—Pennsylvania—Biography. I. Asbell, Bernard, joint author. II. Title.
RC339.52.H37A33   616.8'9'00924 [B]   78-26127
ISBN 0-87223-516-5

8.95/5.73   5/79

To my dad,
Fred W. Hartman
(1918–1978),
who always said,
"You never know
unless you try."

The author is especially grateful to his wife, Cheryl Walker Hartman, for the extensive investments of her time, intelligence, and devotion in every phase of the preparation of this book. It could not have been done without her.

Contents

1	Where's the Real Doctor?	3
2	On Being Blind	11
3	When the World Went Dark	21
4	"Why Can't He Get It Himself?"	30
5	School for the Blind	45
6	Into the World of the Sighted	57
7	Blind Dating	67
8	Getting Hooked on Medicine	83
9	Wayne	88
10	Anybody Around?	98
11	Love Is Blind	108
12	The Last I Remember Was Three Rusty Nails	121
13	A Freshman on Broad Street	150
14	Getting Through	161
15	Looking Back	169
16	And Now the Story Begins	180

WHITE COAT,
WHITE CANE

❊❊ 1 ❊❊

Where's the Real Doctor?

This woman I'm on my way to see, no doubt by now she's bared her knees and thighs, and she's going to put her hands in mine and try to tease me into doing something I don't think I want to do. I'm terrified. I feel too inexperienced for deciding yes or no.

The woman is seventy-five. She's sharp of mind with a tongue of jagged glass. Crabby too, but that's easy to forgive because every joint in her creaky frame aches, practically all the time, or so she says. And she detests doctors, *all* doctors, sight unseen.

"How're you doing?" I greet the arthritic old woman in a small consulting room just off the hospital outpatient clinic.

"Fine," she lies, grumpily. The source of that syllable tells me she's seated, and I take my place behind a small desk at a memorized location to her left. Taking her hands, I lightly touch her fingers, then her knees, wondering if she recognizes me. Last week when we first met I was just an observer, tagging along on the rounds of John Martin, a doctor two or three years older than I and my mentor in the current focus of my training, rheumatology.

"What are you doing?" the woman challenges. "You're blind."

"I'm examining you. Haven't you ever seen a blind doctor before?"

She refuses to be humored. "I don't see what a blind doctor can do."

"I'm not sure either, but we're going to find out."

The lady doesn't know how handicapped I *really* am, and it has nothing to do with being blind. The real handicap is that I'm green as a nine-dollar bill. And scared. Only a few weeks have passed since I answered the call of my name and mounted a platform at Temple University to be handed a parchment scroll that changed me forever from Dave Hartman to David W. Hartman, M.D. Overnight the newspapers and broadcast news made me a minor celebrity, the first blind person in a hundred years to be admitted to a medical school, eventually to become a doctor. I received letters and awards and handshakes and a few kisses and a lot of admiration from old friends and neighbors. The compliment I heard most often, said either directly to me or to others, was that I must be brilliant. Every time I hear that, my nerves twitch. I try not to get mad.

I am not brilliant. Medical training depends largely on memory, and like most students I have to struggle to memorize anything. I have a lousy vocabulary, and can show test scores to prove it. What it took to get me through—into medical school as well as out of it—was not genius but sixteen grinding hours a day to review on tape, or finger in Braille, what sighted students could study in eight or ten. Saying that I "must be brilliant," saying that I am an exception, perpetuates the assumption that blind people are—and ought to be—helpless, hopeless, and pitiable, and incapable of higher training, such as medical school. That assumption is so deeply ingrained that it's coaxed blind people indeed to conform as helpless, hopeless, and self-pitying. A blind person who qualifies should not have to prove he or she is a genius to be given an opportunity for higher training.

But to get back to my predicament, the decision I have to make about this woman is embarrassingly elementary, and I feel dumb for making such a big deal of it. Oh, God, grant me two little years of experience, even a year, so my palms don't sweat with indecision and ignorance every time I have to say yes or no. Just this morning a ward patient complained to me that his itchy behind was driving him crazy, and examining him, sure enough, I fingered ripe, juicy hemorrhoids. Searching my teeming head, I realized that I could play back volumes of what our professors taught us about the cardio-vascular system and the latest theories in immunology, but they never told us what to give for hemorrhoids. I asked my floor's most experienced nurse. With a shrug in her voice she said, "I can tell you what my husband takes." I phoned the pharmacy to send up what her husband takes.

Look, God, I can't wait for a year's experience. Just help me get this old woman to quit blaming my blindness for my ignorance. It rattles me when I'm trying to make this ludicrously simple decision: She wants an injection for her pain, but won't give me any information to justify it. *Should I give it to her?* As you'd expect an arthritic's joints to be, her fingers are gnarled and crooked, her knees lumpy rocks. But I feel no swelling, no sign of an irregular flare-up. I press here, there, trying to rouse an inflamed spot.

"All over," she keeps moaning. "It hurts all over. Where's the doctor?"

"I'm the doctor."

"I mean the real doctor, the one I saw last week."

Maybe she's right. Maybe I'm not a real doctor if I can't even coax out of her where she hurts. Now she's heaving dramatic gusts of breath. Through a stethoscope I hear nothing in her lungs to account for them. I'm afraid she's going to die. John, where the hell are you now that I really need you? I must send for John. John unexpectedly bustles through the door.

He's as puzzled as I am. I feel a flutter of secret satisfaction. John decides as I already have: no injection. After soothing the old woman and sending her off to her physical-therapy workout, John and I discuss a theory. When she's about to see a doctor she gets nervous and starts to breathe hard. Rapid breathing can change the pH of the blood, make it more acidic, and may bring on some strange symptoms. These symptoms, called the hyperventilation syndrome, may include numbness of the fingers and face, and all sorts of discomfort. It's the most reasonable guess we can make. A lot of medical decisions are guesswork. Corroboration by my mentor—and suddenly I don't care that it was such a simple decision—makes me feel like Christiaan Barnard. Maybe I *will* be a real doctor.

A few minutes later, up on my floor, I'm slapped in the face by a thought: *behind* her knees; I never checked underneath for swelling or inflammation. I've got to take that elevator and see her again.

Then a second later: There's no way there's going to be fluid behind those knees when there was none elsewhere. I turn back.

Then a second later: Gosh, I have extra time now. I should check it. Again I swing my white cane around and head for the elevator.

Then a second later: This is obsessive-compulsive. I can't go through a career like this, worrying about the unnecessary when the days will get ever more crowded with necessaries, imperatives. The time to start learning to relax is right now. I turn back.

Then a second later: The way to relax is to go back there. There's no sense going through the weekend worrying about whether or not I should have checked behind that woman's knees. Anyhow, a good doctor *should* be obsessive-compulsive; the ones who aren't are the ones who let symptoms slip through the cracks. I go for the elevator.

There's a hand on my elbow. The solicitous voice of our kindliest woman patient asks, "Doctor, are you lost?"

I'm about to say no. Then I'm about to say yes. I laugh and tell her, "I'm trying to make up my mind."

I head for the elevator.

Behind the woman's knees I find nothing.

It's like a different world several weeks later when I get a phone call on my ward floor to hurry downstairs to physical therapy—one of my ward patients is stricken with chest pains. The patient is a black woman of sixty-one who recently suffered a stroke. I find her lying on the floor, holding her belly. What's going on? Are they chest pains or belly pains? Her poststroke brain impairment prevents her from answering; in fact, whether she grasps my question is doubtful. Abdomen or chest? This woman urinates through a catheter. If the tube is blocked, her bladder would distend and that could account for her abdominal pain—if it *is* abdominal pain. I need a nurse and, for stripping the patient's clothes off, a place more private than the middle of a gym floor. "Get a stretcher," I instruct a physical therapist, "and get the patient up to her room *stat*." "Stat" is hospital talk for immediately.

When we get upstairs a nurse checks out the catheter. It's okay. Too bad. I'd rather have a blocked plastic tube than a blocked artery. Sure enough, the nurse tells me the woman is now pressing her chest. I tell her to order oxygen, two liters a minute, on standby, and an electrocardiogram (EKG) *stat*. I listen to the patient's heart. Fairly regular. Pulse, good. Blood pressure, no alarms. Her lungs sound noisy at the bottom, not good. She remains fully conscious, but still in pain.

If there's any reasonable chance this is a heart attack, I

shouldn't be in full charge. No first-year resident should. I put in a call for a more experienced resident, a third-year doctor. This particular resident, whom I won't name, is very sure of himself. Which has advantages. And dis-advantages.

The moment he appears I say, "I think we ought to get a blood gas."

"I don't think so," he snaps.

He reviews what I've done so far and grunts approval. I've felt comfortable and secure in handling the emergency. Since starting med school, and since becoming a doctor, I've wondered with a trace of dread how I'd behave in handling my first heart attack. Here it is—maybe—and I haven't panicked, I haven't botched it. I knew what to do and did it.

I repeat, "I think we ought to get a blood gas."

A "blood gas" is a lab test to make sure the blood is circulating well enough to distribute sufficient oxygen to the tissues. Blood has to be drawn by puncturing a major artery, a tricky maneuver. My boss advances some guesses that the patient's problem might be this, or it could be that, but then it might be—

I say, "The only way we're going to know is if we get a blood gas."

After a hesitation he asks, "Can you draw blood gases?"

I say, "Yes."

He says, "Okay. Maybe we'd better."

A lot of doctors are nervous about doing blood gases if they're not highly experienced at it because the artery is often hard to find—by looking. I don't have that prob-lem; I feel for it, press the needle alongside my finger, and slip it in. (Touching the needle is irregular, so for sterility I first rub my fingers in alcohol until they're almost numb.) Lord knows, I'm no whiz at taking blood gases, but I've gone for four arteries and hit two at first try. Fifty percent is a respectable rate. The two I missed belonged to an elderly woman who'd had the procedure numerous times and her thick scar tissue concealed her artery. Also elderly patients often have harder arteries and the needle may slip off the side instead of going through.

So here is this senior resident shying away from a blood gas because he's afraid he may mess it up—not an uncommon decision—then agreeing to it because I, a first-year man, say I'll do it. That shot to my self-esteem doesn't exactly ruin my day. And it's a damn good thing he changed his mind anyway. If we didn't do it and the patient's symptoms later demanded the taking of a blood gas—quite likely as this case develops—we'd have to remove the oxygen supply for at least a half-hour to allow the patient's blood oxygen to return to its own unsupported level. That could be a great risk. Anyhow, we get the patient through—and we get *me* successfully through my first heart attack.

When people ask what kind of doctor I plan to be, my first answer is "brain surgeon." That's when I find out if their curiosity is serious or just polite. After they recover, I report I'm going into psychiatry. Always there's a sigh: At least I won't kill anybody. But not to let the questioners off too easily I'm tempted to remind them that my med school training, my medical degree, and my license to practice were not custom-made for a blind doctor. I went through—and got through—what everyone goes through.

At this point let me set one fact straight. I am not in that halfway-handicapped category of partial sightedness called "legally blind." I am *blind*, as totally as one can be. When I was eight, the retinas peeled off the back of my eyes. That made them as useless—indeed as dead—as burnt-out bulbs in a pair of table lamps. If a flash of lightning seared across the heavens this instant, I wouldn't know it except for the thunder. But until the age of eight I did see, which makes a great difference in communicating with people who can only think of the world as visual.

For a long time I've told people I planned to be a doctor. Some people tried to be kind by suggesting easier, surer ways of self-fulfillment and of being useful. A few translated their doubts to a question I could not answer: "Yes, but *can* a blind person learn to be a doctor?" If it could be done, I thought I could do it. If it couldn't, at least I'd know, and I thought I could accept that. But I could not accept other people barring me because *they* wanted to avoid the risk.

Of the college teachers and medical educators who gambled with me and on me, did any one of them have the slightest shred of assurance that a blind student—any blind student—could make it through modern medical school? They were as much in the dark as I was.

Now that I am a practicing doctor, I still run into doubters. Among patients. Among my fellow professionals. On some bad days I'm one of them. Every doubter I run into brings me down a notch. But after the blues of slipping a few notches, something stirs up the recollection of all the past discouragers and doubters, the ones who said I shouldn't, or couldn't, study science in high school or college because I'd only fail; the ones who said I couldn't qualify for medical school; the ones who said that even if I could qualify I wouldn't be accepted by a medical school; the ones who warned me against the relentless competition of National Board exams that med students have to survive over and over again (and many don't).

At some point you just tire of doubters and doubting, and you want to just walk away from them and get on with it. And yet they come.

2

On Being Blind

One night at medical school I'm at work with a fellow student in a lab when suddenly he drops his chores and blurts, "Holy smoke, can't wait anymore, I have to go to the bathroom," and dashes out. Not a minute later he returns, frustrated and obviously unrelieved. "Goddammit," he fumes, "the lights wouldn't work."

I can't help but roar with delight. Sheepishly he laughs too, wheels around, and disappears again.

Obviously I made peace a long time ago with groping in the darkness of bathrooms—and the darkness of everywhere else. My dad has often told of a night when I was about ten and my grandparents were visiting, an occasion I always welcomed. The family chatted a while, then I excused myself to get some schoolwork done. After an expectant minute, Grandmother whispered to Dad, "Dave is up there in the *dark*." Dad indulgently smiled. In a moment Grandmother—who had become accustomed to my blindness in almost every other way—snapped to the obvious realization.

Regarding sightlessness in the bathroom, I made my adjustment at the Overbrook School for the Blind in Philadelphia. The boys' johns at Overbrook, like many old-fashioned school johns, had long, wall-mounted, trough-like urinals. The only way I could figure out to make sure I was peeing into it and not on the floor was to stand up close, feeling the assurance of the trough touching my thighs. But that was too close and the stream would splash back on me. I'd walk away with sprayed pants. So I adopted the unmanly manner, which I still practice, of sitting down to pee. Why put up with an unnecessary hassle?

Unless my view of it is altogether distorted, people seem immensely and insatiably curious about what it's like to be blind. I find that surprising, considering how easy it is to satisfy the curiosity. What it's like to be, say, queen of England has to remain a romantic mystery forever to the average person, but to be blind all you have to do is cover your eyes with a blindfold and grope around for a day. Let me describe a few essentials about the experience—at least my experience—of living blind.

First of all, I think and imagine visually. I picture—yes, picture—things and places around me. As I sit here in my Philadelphia apartment I picture this couch along this wall, that chair facing me, that closet door, and, beside it, that door to the hall. On the opposite wall, an air conditioner in that window, and beneath it a table. As I look around the room I see them. Call it a form of pretending if you like. But they're all as real to me as to someone made aware of them by picking up light rays.

My dreams are visual. The people and things of my dreams, the actions that take place, make visual impressions on me, perhaps fuzzier than yours, perhaps in a different mix of auditory and tactile impressions than in your dreams, but essentially visual. But I do not dream of myself as one who can see. In a dream I'm a blind person in a world of sights, just as I'm a blind person in this room that I visualize.

I'm quite sure that my way of dreaming and picturing

would not be experienced by someone who was born blind, who did not have the memory of sight. In the first eight years of my life, although my eyes weren't very good, I did see. My ways of observing, experiencing, and thinking are based on the awareness of what objects look like, of differences in light and color. Very important, my memory of seeing enables me to grasp the abstract idea of a diagram or picture as an artificial representation of something else. As a result, my style of thinking and learning is closer to that of a sighted person than of someone born blind. I have sometimes wondered whether my ambition to be a doctor would have been achievable if I'd been born blind. My best guess is it could be done. In any case, I'll be damned if I'll prejudge other people's capacities the way too many people have prejudged mine. Those prejudgments have unjustly caused me more frustration and anguish than blindness itself.

The importance of experiences missed by a blind person is often overestimated by the sighted. And sometimes it's underestimated.

I have never seen the face of my wife Cheri, or the face of any pretty girl since I was old enough to know that girls are important. But there's no way you can convince me that I am thereby seriously deprived. I don't know what your lover's face does for you, but I don't think that Cheri's face (which I'm told is very pretty) can augment the love I feel through her soft hands, her giving body, her voice that's full of melody and zest and optimism and caring and absolutely devoid of guile. It's important to me, I'll confess, that Cheri is pretty of face, because facial attractiveness is important to other men and I enjoy her being desirable in other people's terms. But I don't comprehend, nor do I really care, what an attractive face—or a homely face—is.

That's probably why I disappoint an occasional acquaintance who, in a burst of proffered intimacy, will say, "Do you want to feel my face? I won't mind." Sorry, but I'm not a face feeler. It means no more than when somebody says, "Oh, too bad you can't see that bee-*yoo*tiful sunset." If I'd lost my sight at the age of seventeen, maybe I'd miss sunsets, but I have no need for sunsets any more than faces.

Colors are something else, quite real in a way—my own way. Certain words, almost all names, even letters of the alphabet, suggest colors. The letter "B," say, is sort of reddish—and, yes, I'm quite sure I remember what red is. If my red is no longer the same as your red, that may bother you, but not me.

To me the word "beautiful" does not connote visual experience. Beauty can be music. Beauty can be the country, its humid perfumes and whispering, gossipy leaves and busy-body birds. Beauty goes beyond hearing and smelling and feeling. It might be a bonfire in the chest, like loving and feeling loved. I'm not sure I'd know how to handle any more knowledge of beauty than I already have. But thanks anyhow.

Much of the time I totally forget that I'm blind. I don't mean that I go around staring at people, thinking that I can see, but I just forget to remember that I'm different. Actually, I don't mind being different. It has benefits. For example, classes in medical school have 200 students. When I go up to talk to a professor after a class, I know he remembers me—or will next time—and he can scarcely help but take an interest in me (even if it's an interest in getting me thrown out of med school).

What reminds me that I'm blind, on the other hand, is the constant, frustrating inconvenience of it. Having to take up a busy nurse's time to read me a patient's chart. Or having to dictate instructions instead of just scribbling them as other doctors do—illegibly, I hear. Or having to expose my silly weak spots. I'm not the only young doctor in that hospital who didn't know what to give for the first case of hemorrhoids he came across. But I'm the only one who had to ask. Any of my colleagues would have gone straight for the PDR (*Physician's Desk Reference*), a fat book with all the answers, looked it up quickly and secretly, and given a high-sounding, authoritative instruction, never hinting that he was as hemorrhoid-dumb as I was. But I had to *ask*, which stripped me as naked as that patient's behind. Then, to be properly responsible, I had to ask that nurse to double-check by looking up her "prescription" in the PDR, which not only confirmed for her my stupidity but established that I didn't trust her, which is worse. Blindness has drawbacks.

If there's any reason I wish I could see it would be so I could drive a car. Even a bike. I'd like to go home from work without having to call Cheri. She, too, has a demanding career—working toward a Ph.D. in educational psychology and teaching it—that is just as important to her as mine is to me. Or I'd like to get back and forth without having to take the damn city bus, a trip I find just humiliating. To get from the entrance of the hospital to the bus stop involves crossing a few scary corners, including getting across Broad Street, which just terrifies the life out of me. Maybe if I'd grown up in the big city instead of a suburb, getting around these streets would be easier, but it's the most hair-raising experience I know. I've learned the exact technique for standing on a corner looking pathetic until someone offers help. Once across I have to stay close to the buildings so I won't angle off the edge of the sidewalk into the horns and screeching tires of Broad Street. I walk at a crawl and feel embarrassed by it. I wish I could walk briskly the way I can hear others do.

When I finally maneuver those crossings to the bus stop, I need to get some Good Samaritan's attention to tell me if it's my bus or not (half the time losing the Good Samaritan because *his* bus arrived first, so now I have to find another Good Samaritan), then survive the crowd that storms the bus. Finally I'm inside, coins in hand, triumphant—and I miss the coin box and my money drops to the floor. I feel like a blind idiot. I visualize everybody laughing at me, except the ones gaping with pity, and I can't stand either.

When this happens on the way home, I'll just say something like, "Goddamn bus!" and Cheri knows exactly what I mean and I feel better. But in the morning, on my way to the hospital, it can bust up my day. Nurses talk about doctors who have those days when their wives burn the toast, or didn't come across the night before. If a nurse really knows me, she probably whispers, "Uh-oh, he missed the slot for his dime again." I don't like walking into a patient's room feeling stupid, incompetent, the blind dunce who can't find the coin slot. But then some patient says he feels better than yesterday, and thanks *me* for it, and I slip back into the doctor feeling, a half-notch more competent than God.

The worst of it is not the dependence or the wasted time, but that it makes me *feel* blind—feel like the popular image of the blind. And I hate that image. Not only for what the sighted see in it but for the way it makes the blind see themselves: the tapping white cane, the tin cup, the ancient picture of poor wretches by the side of the road, wailing, "Alms for the blind." The blind beggar, like one word. The Bible, New Testament and Old, is merciless to the blind. When Christ goes out to prove his divine powers by healing a blind man, of course his beneficiary is a blind beggar, one word. And doesn't the phrase "the blind leading the blind"—the essence of helplessness and aimlessness—come from the Bible? Then think of what *Treasure Island* does to growing kids and the formation of their regard for the blind. The character who brings the black spot of death is a blind beggar—a *pirate* blind beggar, at that. In stories for children, why is disability, like Captain Hook's missing limb, so often connected with evil?

Besides wishing I could drive a car or ride a bike, I do wish I could pick up a book and read it in an evening or

two, as fast readers do. And I wish I could play baseball—
be a pitcher. But I have a neat way of controlling that
fantasy. I know that if I could be a pitcher, I'd then want
to be a great pitcher, a star, the hero of the team; and if I
could do that, I'd want to be an immortal hero. So no matter what, you wind up frustrated. I sometimes convince
myself that I'm no worse off, really, staying home, listening
to the Phillies on the radio.

I'd like to play tennis. Cheri plays tennis every chance
she gets and I really wish I could play with her. I've played
table tennis but, needless to say, not well. I'm quite sure I
have this memory of seeing tennis played when I was very
young, because I have this beautiful image in my head of
people gracefully sweeping across the court. With Cheri,
that would be even more fun than dancing.

I really wish I could see a skin flick. Cheri and I recently
spent a weekend—we call it our sex weekend—at a work-
shop for doctors, ministers, social workers, and such, along
with their spouses, directed at helping the "helping pro-
fessions" talk freely and easily with their clients about sex
and sex problems. You might be surprised at how difficult
talking about sex is for most doctors. As a way of loosening
us up and reducing our shock regions, we spent a long evening watching filmed body operas that were notable not
only for what the bodies were doing but sometimes for
the number and gender of the bodies doing the doing. Cheri
would describe to me what was going on, but she's first to
admit that seeing it is more fun.

I've been asked if my sex fantasies are visual. Damn
right they are. I visualize nudes. But I'd rather see them
for real. Sometimes I compensate by reading (with Cheri)
a particularly descriptive sexy book. I enjoyed *Fanny Hill*.

During that weekend, after being saturated with the films,
we talked about what we saw. One supercilious smartass
kept saying how boring they were. Well, maybe being bored
is an effective way to suppress desire and frustration and

fear of not making it with lovers, but I felt sorry for him for having to go that way.

I know this game of I-wish-I-could-play-this-or-see-that is misdirected regret. If I could see I'd probably have a burning in the breast for some kind of personal recognition, like being on television. If I could see I wouldn't have had the thrill of being the subject of a two-hour special on NBC about my struggle to get into medical school, which I hope changed some people's feelings about the blind, and, even more, I hope it changed some blind people's feelings about themselves.

Sometimes I feel that everything and anything I ever achieve will be linked inseparably to my blindness, the blindness being more important than the achievement—or the achiever. "Did you hear what that blind doctor's done now? Yeah, wow, blind!" Someday I'd like to do something totally independent of blindness, something that might be written about, without the writer saying that this guy can't see. I hope someday to accomplish that.

All those physical hassles brought on by blindness are frustrating, they generate flashes of self-pity, but you cope with them. The part you never get used to—at least I don't—is dealing with new people, new social situations. For example, I love partying, but I'm always uncomfortable at parties, especially when new people are around, and especially during the first few minutes. No, it's not because I'm sensitive about being the only blind person in the room. I'm not. What I worry about is *me*, my personality, whether I'm doing something out of place.

Sure, that's the same worry everybody has. I never understood the special reasons for my special worry, however, until reading a remarkable book, *The Making of Blind Men*, by Robert A. Scott, a Princeton sociologist whose studies about the life and world of the blind helped me crystallize what I'd been feeling. Sighted people in a sighted world develop a complex system of messages, cues, and feedback signals that tell each party in an encounter what's going on and how to deal with the other. Those signals don't have to be visual, but sighted people in a sighted world are so accustomed to relying on visual signals that they cannot easily shift to another system.

First, there's the simple business of two people sizing each other up. That guy's dressed to kill—diamond ring, $500 suit. You just know he's a big success some way or another and you start dealing with him in a certain way, probably with respect, whether you respect him or not. Some other guy is dressed shabbily, but he's young and exudes brightness and curiosity. You respect him in a different way, and act differently with him.

The second point is the sighted person's discomfort at encountering a blind person. That successful guy senses his $500 suit isn't doing what he paid for it to do, and he feels naked. Or I've had a girl say to me, after a few minutes of a tense first encounter, "You must think I'm weird. I have a froggy voice." Girls realize that they're suddenly all voice, that the necklaces and bracelets, the lipstick and painted nails, the big boobs and fluttering eyelids, no longer count, and they're lost. They don't know who they are, or don't know who *I* think they are, and they can't stand it. The peril of it works two ways. I made a mistake with the girl of the froggy voice. Because it was all I knew about her, and just to tease, I began calling her "Froggy." Soon I realized she was upset, defensive, dripping with icicles. To have teased her repeatedly for being flat-chested or hairy would have been just as brutal.

The third cue-and-response problem is when a blind person enters the presence of a group of people and fails to sense immediately what's going on so he can act appropriately. I may bust in, feeling good, and make a wisecrack. If I could have seen their solemn faces I'd have known their mood was serious or hostile or downright somber—maybe someone's mother just died. I keep resolving to learn to shut up on entering a room, listen, pick up the mood, then join in appropriately, but that kind of reserve just isn't my nature.

My most memorable case of inappropriate response was at a social event at Temple University when a friendly male voice said, "Hi, I'm Guy Chan, how are ya?" "Fine," I responded, pumping his hand, "glad to seeya, Guy." Then, suddenly, it clicked. *Dr.* Chan was the maybe fifty-year-old chairman of the department of ophthalmology! What to do? Go back and say, "Sorry, Dr. Chan, that I called you Guy"?

I have to be especially careful on my floor when talking to another doctor or a nurse about a patient and his or her condition, first making sure no one else is around. I learned that at med school, not through a lecture on confidentiality but just on my way to class one morning. I pushed into a crowded elevator carrying a cup of coffee in each hand. "Up all night again, Dave?" a fellow student joshed.

"No, but I'm afraid I may have another good night's sleep in Professor You-know-who's class."

None of the students around me snickered. What a disappointment. I thought it was a good line. Just then the doors opened to my floor and someone behind me, eager to get out first, pushed past, growling, "Excuse me, Hartman."

Unmistakably, it was the voice of Professor You-know-who.

✕✕ 3 ✕✕

When the World
Went Dark

I can think of one doctor with a perfectly good pair of
eyes who, in a sense, was blind. When I was less than two
years old, my mother took me on a routine trip to a pediatrician. I must have bothered him. As my mother tells it,
I crawled around the floor reaching for this and that. If he
put down something—a jar, a wad of cotton, a tongue de-
pressor—I'd reach for it, almost sticking my nose into it.
Finally the doctor scolded her: "You're going to have an
awful problem with this child. You'd better start right now
teaching him not to touch everything he sees." My gentle-
hearted, oversensitive Mom felt demolished, disgraced as a
mother.

That doctor was being handed, ready-made, a gorgeous,
perfect diagnostic clue. Did he expect a two-year-old to
give him a written medical evaluation, complete with ref-
erences? That kid—*I*—was saying something loud and
clear and clinically significant. And the doctor's only response was annoyance.

Then one day during a family get-together my Uncle
Chill—Dr. Charles Harms, Mom's brother—told my parents that my eyes simply were not working right. Rather

than examine me closely himself in something that was not his specialty, Uncle Chill suggested that Mom get me to the clinic of the Wills Eye Hospital in Philadelphia.

What the doctors at Wills found was that I could see fairly clearly for only an inch or two in front of my nose. They further discovered I had been born with spherical lenses, caused by a weakness of the eye muscles that prevents the lenses from being stretched into their proper bowl shape. The lenses of the eyes, as in a camera, focus light. If they're out of shape, you still see, but through a frustrating blur. (The lenses should not be confused with the retina, which corresponds to the film. Without film in a camera, there cannot be a picture. Without a retina, there's no sight.)

Then and there, the doctors hospitalized me, zonked me out with ether, slit open one of my eyes to remove the misshapen lens, and fitted me with a pair of specs, little more than an inch in diameter for my baby face, the corrective lens being almost as thick as my little finger. Miraculous. It improved my sight to about 20/40—through a range of twelve inches. They would have done the same with the other lens, except they couldn't find it. It was floating around somewhere. The doctors instructed my mother and father how to look for a certain reflection like a drop of oil in that eye—a signal that the wayward lens had suddenly come home—and to rush me, lying on my abdomen, back to the hospital if they saw it.

I broke my tiny glasses twice the first week I wore them —once just from carelessly dropping them; another time when Mom suddenly had to brake her car and I smacked into the dashboard. A third mishap occurred when I was tinkling, probably staring straight down to take careful aim. The damn lens popped out of the frame and right into the toilet. Mom had to fish it out.

One summer day about three years later—I was now five —we were expecting a visit from Uncle Chill, always a particularly happy event for me. My mother has two brothers, both great guys, but maybe it's the fact that Uncle Chill never had a son that made him cultivate a special closeness with me. There's no doubt in my mind that Uncle Chill's being a doctor had a great deal to do with my early vision of myself as a doctor. Anyway, to kill time before his arrival that day, I borrowed my sister Bobbie's bike. Around the corner of our suburban block the bike slipped and I took a mild spill. Thinking little of it, I climbed back on and rode home, but a few minutes later at the lunch table, Mom suddenly peered at me and exclaimed, "The lens! There it is!" She rushed me to the car and to the hospital.

I was overcome by a sense of calamity—not over the impending operation or fear of being hurt by the doctors (I really had no recollection of what they had done to me three years earlier) but because the anticipation of my exciting afternoon with Uncle Chill was—*whoosh*—blown away.

As I recall, one doctor looked at me, then another, then another, different ages, sizes, voices, and I think one had a beard. One of them said resolutely, "Let's get him up to the operating room."

As I lay on the table, the ornery lens slipped away again. They didn't find it.

Childhood was a happy time. Always I felt warmly cloaked—but never smothered—with love from my sister and parents and grandparents and relatives and friends. I knew that that love came to me not because I was their poor, unfortunate kid, but simply because I was me and I was theirs. And that feeling, I believe, is most of what happiness is. So I was a happy kid.

Only one thing deeply troubled me. I had a strong drive to be good, to please others, to avoid disapproval and punishment, but no matter how good I tried to be I'd screw everything up. Or so it felt. At home I'd crash into furniture, knock over lamps. Rubbing my head affectionately, Dad, trying his best to look amused, would tell visitors that I was a light tank.

At age six, same as other kids, I entered first grade at the public school just three doors down from my house in Havertown, Pennsylvania. Our first-grade teacher was on the strict side (and I can't help but smile at saying that, because at the moment this is being told, that dear lady who has become a family friend is a weekend guest of my parents). I'd have to sit in the front row of class so I could see better, but that meant that Teacher would see *me* better. She'd see everything I did.

For my school lunch, every few days Mom would pack her specialty, a terrific egg salad sandwich. There was this one snively kid in my second-grade class who'd usually eat at our table—an older kid who'd flunked a few times and whom nobody liked—and one day he said, "Pheeew! You've got that smelly sandwich again." He'd said that before, and this was once too often. I said, "I'll meet you out back in the playground." I was about seven, with those thick glasses; he was about nine.

I don't remember the fight, except him running away at the end of it. A minute later he came back, accompanied by his big brother, hollering that his head was bleeding. I was sure I was going to be kicked out of school for punching a hole in that kid's head. A male teacher came over—I was terrified—and he decided with a judicial air that since I had busted the kid's head open and he had slightly bent the frame of my eyeglasses we were about even, and he dismissed us both. I wound up with a skeptical regard for that teacher's sense of equity, but I was grateful.

Actually I wasn't very athletic at age seven. I couldn't have been a very fast runner, because I remember clearly a girl in our class who had wobbly legs and knock-knees and ran like a chicken, and another girl who was about three-foot-six and must have weighed 200 pounds, just enormous, and I remember a race when the three of us ran at the same speed. So you know I wasn't a dasher.

But, all in all, I was a happy kid.

In 1957, when I was eight and in the third grade of public school, to add to my difficulties it was discovered that I had glaucoma. Although disturbing to my ophthalmologist, a dear man whom I'll call Dr. Campbell, it was not altogether surprising because glaucoma runs in my parents' families. He prescribed a medication but with a stern warning to my mother that a possible side effect of the drug was retinal detachment, in many ways more serious and less treatable than glaucoma, but highly unlikely, especially if we were vigilant in watching for its early warnings. He told her—and she told me—that if ever I saw "sparks" and began to lose vision we were to stop the medication immediately and hurry to see him. Taking the proper precautions, Dr. Campbell had little choice but to play the odds. It's what doctors are trained to do, and indeed what I would do today under comparable circumstances.

A few weeks later my sight began going dim in my right eye. I didn't say a word, was afraid to. I could tell from Dr. Campbell's warning that if I said anything I might have to go back to that hospital, which meant that awful ether again, and the way to avoid it, obviously, was not to say anything. A few days later, sure enough, I saw those sparks and—my God—the right eye had now gone dark, it saw nothing at all! I panicked and ran to Mom and Dad, who took me to the doctor. I still remember Dr. Campbell flashing that light into my head and the ominous way he said, "Uh-huh." He sent me out to the waiting room and called my parents in. When they came out, I could tell my mother was worried and trembly, and Dad said, "Dave, we're going to put you in the hospital for a while."

I began to cry, not in fear of the hospital but in fear of

being separated from my parents. I remember that the doctor's secretary had her arm in a sling and after a few minutes I asked her what was wrong with her arm. For years later she marveled and reminded me of that incident, always saying that I was such a brave and generous boy for thinking of her injury at a moment when I had so many troubles of my own. I really appreciate her sentiment, but what the incident really illustrates is the limited and easily distractable attention of an eight-year-old.

The operation was scheduled for the day before Christmas. I was nervous all morning, but also relieved. They told me I wasn't going to get ether this time. Instead, they stuck a needle into my arm with sodium pentothal and I went right out in a rush of ecstasy.

Next day, Christmas, there I was, bandages over both eyes, head propped between two sandbags because it was absolutely imperative that I not turn my head. I remember that in the children's ward everybody got three Christmas gifts from the hospital. Mine were a furry stuffed cat, a Slinky, and a wiry circular gadget that you could bend into all sorts of weird shapes that I could feel and that really kept me fascinated. Also I got a table radio from my grandparents and loads of stuff from bunches of other people who kept coming. Only a small number of people, I think four, were permitted in the room at a time, so people would come in and gape and force cheery words and walk out so another group could come in and gape and force cheery words and so forth. I felt like a little king holding court in a sandbag throne. I kept waiting for my sister Bobbie, who is two years older than I, but finally learned she wasn't allowed in because she was too young. I really wanted to see her. Well, only partly did I want to see her. I also wanted her to see me and all the attention I was getting and how important I was.

The attention was exhilarating, but that was only one side of the moon. The other was the terror and loneliness when they all had to leave, of having to go to sleep amid strangers and sandbags, with blindfolded eyes and in total darkness. And then that long morning. They'd wake us up at five, and Mom wasn't allowed in till eleven.

Every morning I'd listen to that gift radio. I learned the voice of every announcer and could identify the station and the hour by the voice. At about ten I'd start listening for Mom's footsteps, which I'd come to know as surely as her voice, and after ten-thirty I'd almost burst listening for them. When I finally heard them, anticipated though they were, their sound was a surprise, something wondrous, a miracle. She'd read me the mail, open my packages, mother me through lunch. In the long afternoon—probably long for her, but not for me if she was there—she'd read to me from a book, or chat, or just sit and be there. At five she'd have to leave for a few minutes, which I didn't mind because it was to pick up Dad. But then they'd go down to get their supper, which was a horrible time. After an interminable half-hour they'd be back and could stay until eight. Eight o'clock was pure hell.

Another unforgettable part of the hospital experience was the daily visit of Dr. Campbell. Next to my mother's, his arrival was the biggest thing in the world. I just worshiped him for his kindliness and his authority. He reinforced the feeling I first gleaned from Uncle Chill that being a doctor is the most admirable and awesome state imaginable.

During that hellish Christmas week the doctors removed my bandages and found that the operation had failed. The retina of my right eye just wouldn't stay stuck in place. To understand the condition, picture the retina as a sort of wallpaper on a wall of microscopic blood vessels. Detachment is like the wallpaper peeling off. It is an extremely serious matter because the retina is thereby cut off from the nourishment of the blood supply and dies, not to mention the pain to its possessor.

Dr. Campbell, then a relatively young ophthalmologist,

hoping to save my eye, was eager to get me to the most experienced retinal specialists available, and that meant the famed retina clinic of the Massachusetts General Hospital. Mom, Dad, and I flew to Boston—my first plane ride—for an examination, leading to the scheduling of another operation in February.

The February operation did not make matters better, but worse. For the first three days in that dank Boston hospital I'd spent hour after hour lying still on a table in a small room where doctors shone lights into my eyes, drawing pictures on a large chart of what they saw, talking and talking about it. They were going through an extraordinarily meticulous preparation for my surgery. After many hours I'd ask, "What time is it?" A doctor would say, "Twenty after two." They had no idea of my distress. Visiting hours had begun at two o'clock. I had already lost twenty precious minutes of the only thing that mattered, the bedside visit from Mom.

The operation finally took place on a Thursday. It lasted five hours. I don't know all the complications the doctors ran into, but apparently the parts of my eye just wouldn't go together right. At the end the retina disintegrated, darkening my right eye forever. The next day, Friday, one of the doctors, a Japanese, came to my bedside and said to my mother, "The glaucoma pressure in his left eye has now gone up extremely high. That retina is bound to detach, too. We have to operate again tomorrow."

Early next morning Mom called Dad with the news. He and Bobbie were home and Bobbie has told me of watching Dad put down the phone, get down on his knees at the dining-room table, and clasp his hands, unabashedly sobbing and saying aloud, "Please, God, please save Dave's sight. Don't let him lose it." A child never forgets seeing a father cry for the first time, and this was Bobbie's first time.

Neither the doctors nor Dad's prayers could save my vision. The retina of my left eye disintegrated, too. I'm sure what the doctors figured was that here's an eight-year-old having his third operation in less than four months. If they had already found it impossible to save the right retina under identical circumstances, a painful and prolonged attempt to salvage the left was scarcely a worthwhile gamble. Why put a kid through hell on a bet of such long odds? I think today that they probably made the best decision. That Saturday, February 15, 1958, the day after Valentine's Day, was the last day that I saw.

4

"Why Can't He Get It Himself?"

One of my first reactions to being blind was glee. I didn't have to wear glasses anymore. Another reaction was dismay. All my young life I'd always had to ride my sister's hand-me-down bikes, but recently Dad had won a prize at the bank he worked for, a big, gleaming boy's Columbia bike, and he'd given it to me, gorgeous and all mine. Now, bam!—just a few weeks later and I couldn't ride it. My Dad tried taking me to a big field where I couldn't slam into anything and wouldn't get hurt if I fell. But it wasn't the same. I could keep my balance on it, could steer it. But if you don't know where you're going, bikes just aren't fun. So that was a vote against blindness.

I was soon to learn that losing my sight had far more serious implications. Still, if you're looking for something that adds up to simple sums justifying simple pity—or simple admiration because I've overcome much of the handicap—that's not the story I have to tell.

Soon after the operation I began going nuts, in a manner of speaking. It started one day when my mother had just driven Bobbie to her weekly half-hour violin lesson, and Mom and I were sitting in the car waiting for Bobbie to come out. Mom was reading to me. I turned my head—don't know why, maybe toward a sound, maybe just fidgetiness—and suddenly I couldn't turn it back. A fantasy, a kind of seizure took hold of me, some fear that my head would only turn in one way, further around, but could not be made to turn back—as though it were on a ratchet—and that if it kept twisting only that one way, it would break off. I cannot exaggerate the helplessness, the pure fright that overcame me, and I began to whimper, then cry, knowing I was not conveying to Mom the degree of my terror. She held me in her arms and before long, though it seemed an eternity, something in my neck relaxed and the nightmare was gone.

Several times over the next few weeks the spasm, the seizure, whatever it was, returned. We tried hot baths to relax my neck. They didn't help. One day I discovered that if I lay on Mom and Dad's double bed, my head between their two pillows, my neck would relax far more quickly than any other way. I tried it on my own bed, and it wouldn't work. I decided at the time—being too young to consider the obvious symbolism—that my mother's bed was warmer because the angle of the sun's rays hit it, though today I am skeptical of that simple explanation.

Finally a marvelous lady pediatrician told Mom that I needed to get active. Dr. Campbell, hearing my parents mention that I'd been beseeching them for a dog, suggested, "Maybe that would be an answer. Maybe he needs some companionship."

For years I have struggled to try to explain to myself—as well as to newspaper and television interviewers who keep looking for a pat, one-paragraph explanation—the source of my apparent stubbornness, a persistence, some drive that made me fight my teachers, a raft of admissions officers, a portion of the medical profession, even my parents, in a bullish determination to get into medical school and become a doctor. I wish I could offer some elevating and inspirational explanations. But the story of how I got the dog hints at an early pattern of persistent brattiness long before I was blind.

As a little fellow of four or five, I was twice the happy possessor of a dog, but neither pet had fared well. I have the distant recollection that one was cranky from a broken leg that had never been reset while the other pooped all over the house. On losing that second one, I began a campaign for a third, and if you didn't know me as a kid, you can't possibly know what that means. I knew how to find and exploit every opening. My parents had grown afraid to walk into a store with me. I'd ask for this plaything, for that. They learned to say automatically, "No, it costs too much and look at the toys you already have."

When I was seven I remember seeing the most fantastic, irresistible boat model. I ran home and passionately announced, "Mom, I really *want* that boat." She asked, "Do you have any money in your penny bank?" Not enough. So I bit my lip, wished I had it, knew somehow I'd get it, and, sure enough, along came the exploitable opportunity.

I had to have a glaucoma test. When you're very young, too undisciplined to keep your eyes still so they can test the pressure, they have to put you to sleep. In the hospital clinic they put a huge mask on my face and told me to blow up this balloon, filled with ether. I knew what was in it and what was going to happen, and I diligently took deep breaths because I wanted to get the damn thing over with. When I awoke I vomited all over the room. Mom, just dripping with pity and guilt, said, "I think we ought to go out and buy you something."

I got the marvelous, coveted boat—a loser of a boat, as it turned out, because I could never get the glue to hold the pieces together properly.

Another example was my trains. Every year, putting up my electric trains was a big deal for Christmas, except every year I was too impatient to wait that long. In Septem-

ber I'd start. "Mom, Dad, help me put up my trains."
They'd resist. They hated the trains because, from the
moment we put them up, all they'd hear was, "Can I buy
this? Can I buy that?" Also, whatever room we'd use to
lay out the trains, for weeks it was goodbye, room. So
there was an annual struggle, my starting about Labor Day,
their wanting to resist till Christmas Eve, a compromise
being struck somewhere around Armistice Day. My persistence, which might be amusing to read about, was not
amusing to live with. My parents called me "the broken
record."

I'm sorry to break the news to my dear parents that the
way I carried on was partly their fault. I learned this in
college—in Psychology 101—reading about rats. If you
put a rat in a cage, show him how to press a lever, and feed
him a drop of water every time he presses it, he'll press
and press until he's had enough water. If you cut off the
water supply and he presses and presses repeatedly, each
time getting no water, he eventually gets the hint, stops
pressing, and probably lies down and goes to sleep.

But then—aha!—there's the alternate reward system.
Sometimes you give him water and sometimes you don't.
The rat presses the lever. You give him water. He presses
again. You give him another drop. He presses again. You
don't give him any. Presses again. A drop. The next three
times he presses, no water. He's about to quit, presses one
last time—and you give him a drop. Keep doing that and
the rat will never quit pressing.

What I was taught, and must say was taught exceedingly
well—through the alternate reward system—was *never* to
quit. Anybody who thinks that my impetuous, relentless
drive is some intellectual resolve to overcome a physical
handicap is thinking a sweet inspiring thought, but it has
very little to do with me, and almost nothing to do with
my blindness. In fact, my drive probably has more to do
with my sister than anything else.

I discerned early that whenever Bobbie got something that cost money out of a tight family budget, my parents' ability to buy stuff for me suffered. Bobbie and I were in fierce competition, and she had the advantage because she was older—therefore, smarter. Then I discovered *my* advantage. I was always going to doctors, to hospitals, taking ether and vomiting, getting my eyes bandaged and getting lots of sympathy from relatives and friends and my parents, who'd all say, "My gosh, he's going into the hospital again. What can we do for Dave?"

Sure enough, on the day, soon after I lost my sight, when Dr. Campbell said, "Maybe he needs some companionship," the needle was poised at exactly the right spot in the broken record. I instantly renewed my plea for a dog.

So I got Prince. Prince was a cross between a German shepherd and a collie. I just adored that dog, just loved feeling him. I think he dreaded my approach because I would maul him, tousle him, kiss him, drive him nuts. And I swear, that first summer, I think I saw him. If the light hit him strongly, I could see him—not what he looked like, but his coloring. Maybe it was my imagination. But maybe it's possible that some fragments of my retina were still in place and at work, and through them I caught shadings of Prince.

Seeing Prince—or thinking I did—was a precious experience because it fortified my belief that I would soon see again. Two months after my operation I had become a day student at Overbrook School for the Blind in preparation for Monday-to-Friday residence the following school year, as required of all totally blind students. An Overbrook teacher singled me out for special attention and friendship, taking me for walks and giving me candy. One day he said, "A friend of mine who lost his sight prayed every day to get it back. Sure enough, one morning he woke up and could see a little better; next day, still better; another day, better yet. Just by praying."

That impressed me deeply, especially since my parents emphasized religion in my upbringing. So every night, after reading my Bible in Braille, I would add to my string of prayers a plea to see again. (I kept doing that for several years until realizing that destroyed retinas are quite final even for Him, and that God works in subtler, more round-about ways: giving me sight in the sense that He enabled me to get into medical school.) Besides prayers, I undertook to show Him my faith was earnest. After school I'd run up and down our driveway, proving to Him I wasn't scared of crashing into a tree. Actually, being a basic chicken, I didn't run very fast, just enough to impress Him, while hoping He would have no idea of my terror.

One day another teacher mentioned something that would be required of me next year when I'd be a residential student. I replied, "I won't be here next year." She asked, "Why not?" I said, "My sight will be coming back." She said with annoying firmness, "Your sight's not coming back." "Yes it is," I argued, but she wouldn't budge.

That night I pouted to Mom, "I had an argument with a teacher. She just wouldn't believe that I won't have to sleep over at Overbrook next year because I'll be able to see again."

I was sitting on my bed, and Mom was in her room a few feet around the corner. Mom said, "No, that's not true."

Of course, she didn't understand about my teacher's friend, about my praying every night, and my whole plan with its perfectly inevitable result. First thing I knew, I heard Mom crying.

Recently, when all of us—Mom, Dad, Bobbie, and I—exchanged recollections of how I learned I was to be sightless forever and who told me and when, none of us remembered it the same way. Mom, recalling that bedroom-to-bedroom conversation, was sure I had been told earlier, but she couldn't remember when or how. Dad said he was sure he'd told me. Bobbie remembered some other, more complicated version.

That would all be very puzzling except for my experience as a doctor at the hospital. I've seen this several times: A patient has cancer, and the doctor goes in and says forthrightly, "I know how hard it is to receive this news, but I have to tell you we found a tumor." Three days later, someone else comes in and announces, "We've decided to treat your cancer with chemotherapy." The patient protests, "Nobody told me I had cancer!" The first doctor, using the word "tumor," not "cancer," was trying to soften the blow—for himself as well as the patient—with a slightly oblique euphemism, and the patient grasped the opportunity to miss the dreadful point—to not hear.

I clearly remember my immediate reaction to the finality of what Mom said. For years I felt guilty about that reaction and, until recently, would not have dared mention it to anybody. I knew a heavy thing had been dropped on me and knew I should probably start crying or something, but I was overcome by a peculiar thrill. *Everybody's going to feel sorry for me now. I'll be everybody's little angel and they'll all pay attention. I'll get a lot of presents.* Also I could now go out and solemnly drop on my friends this heavy, heavy piece of information.

A few pages back I speculated that my bullheadedness (which some may call ambition) is attributable to the special ways my parents egged me on. There's another important aspect to this: the way they consistently encouraged me to go out and *do*, unlike many parents in the same position who nurture in their blind kids dependence, fear, helplessness, the self-image of a cripple. Those parents later justify themselves by pointing out that their poor dear thing *has* turned out to be a helpless cripple, so weren't they right all along?

Of my two parents, Mom is the more gentle and cautious. Left alone, she might have held me on a pretty tight leash, more fearful that I might get hurt than that I might grow up deprived of robust experience. Or so I thought until recently. In talking with her to prepare for this book, she told me of hours and days when I'd roam a big space behind our house and our neighbors' houses, gamboling on playground equipment, leaping about as an imagined athletic star, running, climbing, cutting up; and all the time I was doing those things, free and unsupervised, Mom was sitting at the back bedroom window, doing her sewing or whatever, just keeping an eye on me. I never knew, and therefore was not inhibited by her watching me. Other parents, take note.

Dad was of a different stripe entirely. When he got home from the bank, if I didn't immediately challenge him to a wrestle, he'd challenge me. Over the years, however, his techniques changed. As my size approached his, whenever I almost had him pinned, he'd suddenly say, "Oops! Watch the lamp." He was never a willing loser. We belonged to a summer swimming-pool club, and Dad was perfectly game for my doing the high dive—which he came to regret.

I should point out that before I lost my sight, when I had all those delicate problems of straying lenses, I was sternly forbidden to indulge in certain shock-prone activities: no horseback riding, no diving, no rough sports of any kind. As soon as my retinas disintegrated, however, all hope of saving my sight was gone, so such restrictions were pointless. I leaped into everything, relishing the relief of it. Not many of my friends yearned to go horseback riding, but I did, only because I previously couldn't. I nagged for three years until I got on a horse. (No fun at all; I never cared about doing it again.)

For exactly the same reason I wanted to leap off the ten-foot-high diving board. Dad said bravely, "Sure, I'll lead you up the ladder and out to the end of the board." I was a little nervous, sensing and respecting each of those ten feet, but took my leap. I'd seen fancy diving and, imitating what I'd seen, I hit the drink flat on my belly, smarting from top to toe. But it was a keen thrill. Dad met me at the rim of the pool, led me up those steps again, and out the length of the board. After a few times, a feeling overtook him: "Gosh, here I am helping my blind son do the high dive, then I climb back down the ladder. That must look great." Standing up there on that pedestal, all our friends watching, he realized he had to take that dive. At his great splash, I hollered, "Dad, that looked great. Do it again." So poor Dad had to do it twice.

Suddenly I was no longer forbidden to play football, either, the surprising thing being that the neighborhood kids let me into their games. I'd play quarterback, and excelled in what came to be known as the Hartman Sneak. I'd step back to heave a pass, everyone screaming my name —all pure deceit—then confound the opposition by running with the ball. Most of the time I'd run in the right direction toward our goal. Sometimes it wasn't touch football but a serious tackling game, and those guys weren't bashful. A few Hartman Sneaks and they made honest tries at killing me. The bewildered foe would finally catch on and our captain would have to say, "Time to get a new quarterback." I wasn't a star, but it was fun and I learned what football feels like.

Then there was baseball. At Overbrook we played a modified game in which a kid with no sight at all, like me, would get down on his knees to bat. The almost-blind pitcher would zip the ball along the grass, you'd hear it and try to time your swing. The problem, of course, was that if you hit the ball it rarely had any lift to it.

For baserunning, a blind batter would run in a pair with a partially sighted guy, and for fielding, the rule was that if a totally blind guy just touched the ball, the batter was out. In translation, this really meant that if the blind guy got *hit* with the batted ball, the batter was out. Those sighted guys, eager to win, weren't dummies—they'd line up all the blind guys right in front of the batter. But I wasn't born yesterday. I soon figured out that the closer I stood, the better the chance of getting the ball in the kisser.

One day I was fielding right next to the pitcher when I heard a tremendous whack, then waited to hear the ball hit the grass, to pick up its direction. Nothing. I realized it was a pop-up of colossal loft, and sure enough the next moment, with a stunning thud, it whomped me right in the center of the back. I told those sighted guys where to stick their rule; I was going out to play the outfield.

That business of batting in the position of prayer, or even swinging at the grass, golf-style, was all right in its way, but one day I told Dad I sure wished I could swing at the ball regular. Dad, always positive, said he'd try to pitch into a very small strike zone, and if I could learn to time my swing I could get a good whack at it. Out in back of our house, he'd pitch and pitch, over and over and over, each time yelling, *"Now,"* to time my swing. We'd have to line up some other poor kid to be catcher. Dad got a big bang out of it—or acted like he did. But really it was a game of *his* skill, not mine. The real challenge was not for me to hit the ball, but for him to hit my bat, although I never let on that it was just as frustrating as hitting the ball in the grass. A couple of times, however, I did make contact with a fearful whomp and sent the ball soaring. That was exciting, mainly because it felt like I was doing what everybody else could do, which made the whole thing worthwhile.

Dad also took me fishing and camping and helped me figure out a way to take up archery. Don Jarvis, a close neighborhood friend, had a bow and arrows. Soon other kids got them and, by God, I wanted to shoot a bow and arrow too. By this time, my parents' attitude about my pursuing "crazy" ambitions had changed. Dad now clearly realized it was perfectly normal for me to want to do anything *he* wanted to do as a kid. He and Mom would try to weigh the pluses and minuses and try to figure out the *how* instead of the *whether* of my boyish wishes.

Someone at the bank was an avid archer, and Dad discussed it with him. He realized that the reason archery sounds crazy for a blind kid is that one assumes the kid's going to point the bow in the wrong direction and shoot somebody in the ass. The real problem was how to hit the target, at least some of the time. Dad scavenged up a little ding-a-ling dinner bell and we hung it in front of the target; in fact, precisely in front of the bull's-eye. Through a lever arrangement, we ran another long string from the target to where we stood, about fifty feet away. Dad would pull the string, I'd listen for the bell, get a fix on just where the target was, and shoot. True, I never got a bull's-eye by splitting the bell, but I'd hit the target about one out of five times.

After the first thrills wore off, I began to feel frustrated at not being able to practice my archery independently. So we hooked up that long string to a pedal. By pressing my foot, I could control the ringing of the bell. Another thing that bugged me was that Mom had to chase down those stray arrows. So we devised a way to tie a couple of arrows to strong lightweight string, shoot them, then just sort of reel them back in. One unforgettable time I shot a little too hard, and the force of the shot and the jerk of the string yanked the arrow almost all the way back, the closest anyone ever came to suicide by bow and arrow.

Dad was forever doing weekend carpentry projects in his basement shop and he let me have all the wood I wanted, and my own set of tools. Don Jarvis and I built a hut "clubhouse" in the backyard. Then, when the neighborhood archery craze gave way to a go-cart craze, I wanted to make a go-cart. Dad told me to draw a plan, which I did on a Braille-type drawing kit: You press lines on cellophane against a spongelike backing, and, for reasons I've never figured out, the lines pop up to become raised lines. (This simple invention, standard for blind people's use but little known among the sighted, was my secret weapon in getting through the diagram note-taking of college science courses and medical school.) Dad was somewhat stunned at my bringing him not only a structural drawing, but also a side view and top view of the cart.

The damnable problem of making both the clubhouse and the go-cart was that I kept hammering my fingers into pulp. Dad finally figured out why. A person trained in Braille sees with his fingers. I'd find the nail and keep my finger on top of it till the last instant to inform my hammering hand where it was. Dad taught me to risk missing the nail in order to save my finger.

One Christmas I got an Erector Set, then a Tinkertoy construction set. I couldn't use their books of directions and diagrams for putting various things together, so I had to invent my own things and ways to build them. Compared to these sets, ready-made toys were boring. A couple of years ago my wife Cheri's two young brothers got fancy tracks for racing miniature cars. All they could do was sit and race them, nothing to think about. Life today —in the playroom, in the kitchen, even at the hospital—is so largely based on following directions. What's helped me is that I've been forced to work things out.

I also got a chemistry set and, since I couldn't read the "cookbook" that came with it, my parents' hearts were often in their throats. It turned out to be relatively harmless, but did lead to my first major medical research project, which came near to killing us all. For a school science project I decided to do research on my hamster, setting out to learn what happens when a hamster becomes an alcoholic. Every day I fed him a few drops of gin, observed closely, and took notes. The first noteworthy thing was that it made him pee a lot. As for significant changes in his social behavior, coordination, equilibrium, etc., that was hard to tell because Mom insisted that I keep him locked in his cage. That is, until our trip to Florida—*aha*!

The five of us—Mom, Dad, Bobbie, I, and the lush— left Philadelphia by car at 3 A.M. and eighteen weary hours later approached a narrow bridge near Savannah, Georgia. Bobbie was relieving Dad at the wheel when she let out a primal scream. The animal had got loose and was trying to crawl up her leg. Trying to soothe her hysteria, Dad instructed her to pull over the first chance she got so he could take over. She couldn't, because her scream and her start so alarmed the drunken beast that he hid under the brake pedal and the only way to stop the car was to crush him. By that time we were in the line of cars entering the bridge and it was too late to stop. Holding Mom's hands to reassure her in the back seat, Dad was actively wonder- ing (so he has told me) whether he and Mom could tread water long enough to rescue my sister and me from the harbor below. Family trauma or no, after the vacation I duly wrote up my research paper on the comparative be- havior of alcoholic and nonalcoholic hamsters.

If there's anything that helped me learn to analyze, look for opportunities, develop a plan, and be flexible in shift- ing plans, it was when Dad taught me how to play chess. I was about six or seven, just before becoming blind. Be- sides using a regular chessboard, I had duplicate pieces on a small pegboard, fitting them into its holes, which made it easier to feel and to review the board before each move. Sometimes Dad would blindfold himself, playing the same way I did, and when he'd do that, I'd usually do better against him. He was a tough, tenacious player. I rarely beat him.

Bobbie was a challenger of an entirely different kind, and there's no way I would have developed aspects of my self-confidence and striving without her. How did she work her wonders? By bugging me. Incessantly, or so I thought. Here's an example that became a family turning point.

My paternal grandmother and grandfather, two of the dearest people in my life, had given me my first Braille wristwatch, and one day Mom asked me to show it to our Sunday company. I said, "It's upstairs on my dresser." Mom said, "Bobbie, would you go up and get it?" Bobbie responded, "Why can't he go up and get it himself?"

I could practically hear Mom's gasp of dismay at Bobbie's callousness toward her poor little blind brother. I was pretty put out myself, more from pure laziness than hurt. But she wouldn't go, and I wanted those visitors to admire the watch, so I had to.

Ultimately Mom became convinced that Bobbie's attitude was better for me than her own; that too much was being done for me; that she was falling into some of the same dependence-fostering habits she had deplored in other Overbrook parents. Bobbie caused me no end of trouble.

For example, being two years older than I, Bobbie was old enough to be stuck with a lot of housework, and soon demanded, "Why can't Dave do some?"

"Well, really," my parents would ask, "what can Dave do around the house?"

One Saturday morning, a day that will live in infamy, Bobbie said, "I'll bet he can vacuum."

Always positive—even when I wish he weren't—Dad said, "Dave, why don't you try vacuuming?"

I pushed and pulled that thing, even starting to enjoy trying to get my strokes in parallel, slightly overlapping stripes. Then I'd call, "Bobbie, does it look right?" She'd come in, inspect, and say, "That's pretty good, but you missed under here. Did you do under here?" And I'd admit, "No." She set a pretty high standard for me—actually close to what she'd require of herself—and although I'd never admit it, that's what made me enjoy meeting it.

Then Bobbie complained, "Dave never takes the dog for a walk. It's *his* dog. No reason he can't walk to the end of the street and back."

Soon her prodding took a new turn: not only to relieve herself of chores but to cultivate my independence. Every morning Mom would put out my school clothes. If Mom was sidetracked by a phone call or Dad being late for work, I'd have to wait for my pants and shirt and socks.

One day when I complained about Mom doing something else first, Bobbie said, "Dave, why don't you organize your clothes so you'll know what shirts go with which pants?"

"How in the world can I do that?"

"You can group stuff by colors and learn which colors go with which. You've got to learn it sometime in your life." Later, Mom sewed Braille color codes into my clothes.

After she entered her first year in college, she'd say impatiently to me, "You're going to *have* to be independent. When you get to college nobody's going to do this stuff for you." That became a standard phrase of hers: "You're going to have to be independent." It had a profound effect on me, and, I'm sure, so did her phrase "When you get to college . . ." My going to college seemed to be her unquestioned assumption, and thus became mine.

Bobbie gave me a constantly hard time, and in doing so she did me the irreplaceable service of *expecting* me to be normal, to carry my own load, and, wherever feasible, to do whatever I do as competently as anyone else.

❊❊ 5 ❊❊

School for the Blind

I completed the third grade as a day student at Overbrook, and the following September had to learn to live there, Monday through Friday. Although school and home were less than five miles apart, they could have been on separate continents. At first I was permitted to talk to Mom and Dad on the phone every night, but after a couple of weeks the school discouraged it. Perhaps I sound clingingly dependent on my parents, but please remember I was only eight. And freshly blind. And scared and confused. And separations from my parents had always meant operations and hospitals and ether and the tyranny of visiting hours.

Most "blind schools" require that a sightless child stay night and day, seeing parents only on weekends. Their explanation is that most parents of the blind have a powerful urge to shield their handicapped child not only from danger, but from experience itself. When the child drops his spoon, the parent leaps to pick it up, creating and guaranteeing the child's physical and psychological dependency. The parent, often guilt-ridden about the child's sightless condition, feels an incessant, engulfing urge to atone for it by filling his every need. Unfortunately, all those cushions end up smothering and immobilizing the child. So in theory the school, which views itself as fostering self-reliance and self-esteem, needs undiluted control of the child's development at least for the major part of the week.

Interesting theory, although I incline to favor day schools and summer camps for kids, and counseling for misguided parents. I just wish that schools for the blind had indeed been more challenging as well as more consistent and professional. (I must emphasize that my observations and opinions have to do with my school experience in the late 1950s and early 1960s. They do not necessarily reflect Overbrook or any other blind school today. In the past ten years, many progressive trends have begun to take hold in the field of education of blind children.)

Overbrook had about 350 students, about equally divided between boys and girls. Besides the usual run of classes, twice a day each newcomer had individual instruction in Braille. I loved Braille lessons, not because I had a thing about reading through my fingers but because I had a thing for my Braille teacher, Miss Springer, who glowed with affection and made me want to please her.

Perhaps most vivid in my memory of the faculty, however, is Mr. Chelli, the boys' gym teacher. He was a firm believer (as I later came to be) that blind guys shouldn't be coddled, that a little toughness doesn't hurt and usually helps. He'd call everybody by his last name: "*Hart*man, what are you doing *now?*" The tone scared and somewhat thrilled me. Nobody had ever called me Hartman before, and I secretly hoped he'd never find out I was really just Dave, a kid. He also taught me to wrestle and made me believe I could win. Dad has said that Mr. Chelli was responsible, indirectly at least, for my wanting to do everything completely and just right—out of pure fear. It seems I'd come home at the end of the week and complain to Dad that the partially sighted guys were lucky because while doing push-ups, for example, if Mr. Chelli looked the other way they could just quit, resting up until he gazed their way again. But since there was no way I could know when Mr. Chelli's back was turned, I had to keep pushing and pushing, up and down, huffing and puffing. If I dared let up for a moment, I might hear, "*Hart*man, what are you doing *now?*"

Overbrook devoted itself to ridding kids of behaviors that accentuated their blind appearance. The big taboo was walking with your hands groping in front of you. Other objectionable behaviors of a type commonly called "blindisms" that sightless children often develop are rocking, bobbing the head, constant weaving of the body. Nobody is sure whether these movements derive from a mere lack of grace by those who cannot relate grace to anything visual, or whether they are a form of self-stimulation in lives deprived of visual sensation.

Mr. Chelli, our tough guy in residence, did not philosophize over such puzzles. He'd command, "Stop it, Dolchin, you're making me *sea*sick and I didn't bring my seasick pills!" This kid I'm calling Dolchin walked dragfoot-style, like an infant or a very old man. He'd push one foot forward, then drag the other up to it. I could tell he was nearby just by hearing him—scrape, scrape. Nothing was wrong with his feet or legs, he'd just never seen anyone walk. If he needed to walk fast, he'd walk like a fast infant. While teachers would scold Dolchin to hurry up, none of them to my knowledge ever took hold of the boy's ankles and said simply and sympathetically, "Ed, walk like this."

Gym class is a good place to learn about others. In games, in tumbling, you bump into people, grab their elbows, get feels of who they are. There's one guy I remember who had a funny voice, and one day, bumping into him, I grabbed his arm. Instead of wrapping my fingers around firm biceps, I had this huge handful of flab, like a jellyfish. After all these years, every time I think of him my memory is not of his funny voice or flabby feel nor an impression of a face, because I don't need his face; my memory of him, however, is visual—an image of a jellyfish. Perhaps it's especially vivid because I have an aversion to flabby muscles and excess fat, which are fairly common characteristics among blind kids, who are so often overshielded from physical activity.

Because I had been athletically inclined even as a small child, I had relatively firm muscles. In gym, that brought me a certain deference and respect, status, although my general status was low because I was totally sightless. (We blind kids were held in contempt by the partially sighted kids, who referred to us as "blinks." Blinks, on the other hand, didn't dare have a nickname for the partially sighted.)

The reason kids who could use their eyes enjoyed status was simple and stark: They had power. And nowhere was this power more mercilessly wielded than at the dining table. A kid who could see—even just enough to distinguish the mashed potatoes from the cranberry sauce—had a good chance of being appointed by the housemother to dish out the food. That coveted job carried the additional privilege of having the right to tell everyone else to shut up, a command you obeyed because he who held the serving spoon controlled what was spooned.

I still remember with anguish and a certain tightening of the innards my fourth year at Overbrook. I was in seventh grade and some little squirt in the fifth grade was in charge of me. I could scarcely suffer the little bastard, but out of necessity I did try to be civil.

When the platters would arrive, I'd ask, "Hey, Mike, what are we having?"

With lordly arrogance he'd mutter, "Food."

"What kind of food?"

"Just food. Shut up."

I'd want to kill him, but I had to restrain myself. A simple trick at his command was to take a small spoon of the best stuff, just wipe it around your plate a little so the housemother would think you had a lot of it, then just leave a miserly dab. An even more powerful weapon was the standing rule that we had to eat everything put on our plates. If you hated spinach, as I did, a malevolent spoon wielder could drown you in spinach. So the server swaggered with the high status that comes with holding seven helpless kids by the gonads.

As in any society, status groups at Overbrook were divided into subgroups. If you were stuck in the low-status group of the totally blind, one way to climb into its higher subgroups was by having a sighted friend who would take care of you when you were up against the wall. Not *any* sighted friend, however; some sighted kids were weirdos—spoiled, flabby, graceless, socially out of it, consequently ranking lower than the blind.

When my sister, Bobbie, was about fifteen, on her visits to me she caught the eye of a sighted guy named Ken who was about seventeen. He developed a terrific crush on her—which, of course, put me in with him like gold. I remember sitting on a bench one day in a school area fancily called "the cloister" when some big fat old sighted kid who lived by bullying everybody started bullying me: just abuse and taunting, knowing I couldn't touch him and that if I got back at him verbally he could just pulverize me. Along came my friend Ken, who could see about as well as the bully but was older and bigger. And Ken was just as friendly as could be, greeting the bully with a clap on the shoulder just a little heartier than necessary.

"Hey, how're ya *do*ing! *Huh?* You like my buddy Dave, *huh?*" Then another friendly swipe and another.

I just sat on that bench, loving every moment. The lesson was unmistakable—I was not to be messed with.

Before I had Ken on my side, I had to learn the uses of

diplomacy, which have not served me badly in the years since. In the fifth grade I acquired an enemy, for reasons I could not then figure out. He was a small, wiry, nervy kid with very good sight, good enough to read large print instead of Braille. He almost qualified for public school. I'd heard stories about a horrible home he came from, which perhaps accounted for his loving to torment a bigger, stronger guy—me—over whom he had the advantage of sight. Out of the clear blue in a hallway he'd sneak up on me, sock me, and run. He knew he could smash me any time he wanted, and did. Nothing had ever made me feel so helpless, so impotent. One day, having no choice, I reported him to a teacher, who of course ordered him to stop. An hour later he snuck up to me, socked me, and ran.

I thought of killing him. I knew it would be easy because he was so much smaller—if only I knew when and how to grab the elusive bastard. I developed the more cautious thought of breaking his arm. The way I imagined doing it —I mean actively imagined, virtually hearing the crunch —was simply by seizing his forearm and slamming it across my knee. But then his arm would eventually heal and he'd hit me again. I had to come to terms with him some other way.

One day I found out where he was eating and I just sat down next to him and said, "Listen, I want to talk to you. What are you so mad at me about?" As I recall, he complained that I was a big shot in the dorm, or the housemother's pet, or some damned thing that bugged him. We talked it out and became friends, more or less.

I'd like to have taken care of him in a more direct, manly way, but couldn't. A blind person just can't go around telling people "up yours" whenever he feels like it. I was learning in the most painful way that I was at the mercy of everybody else, except someone equally blind.

Years later I was a senior at Gettysburg College and anguished that one medical school after another refused to take me. A school organization gave a luncheon for Ralph Nader and I managed to sit opposite him at a long table. Conversation turned to my difficulty. He agreed that since my grades were comparable to those of many students getting into med school, clearly what was keeping me out was that I was blind. "You know," Nader said, "I think we can make a case out of it. We might be able to fight it legally and get you into a medical school."

I was elated. I promised to get to work on a letter to him right away, incorporating all the salient facts. I never prepared the letter. I soon realized that even if Nader and a court could get me in, the school could soon flunk me out if it wanted to. I would be as much at the school's mercy as I was at that hateful kid's. Winning a case is not always the way to win. I decided to do it my way.

So the almost-blind lord it over the blind, and the muscular blind lord it over the flabby blind, and the befriended blind lord it over the friendless blind, and the hierarchy keeps descending, probably to infinite depths.

No matter how blind kids arranged themselves into complex hierarchies to rule over and be ruled by other blind kids, where ultimate power resided was unmistakable and unquestioned. It lay with the housemother. And I suppose housemothers, too, had their power pyramid. If so, there's no doubt in my mind that the pinnacle was occupied by one unforgettable soul I'll call Mrs. Reinhold, who, I'm sorry to say, for a time was *my* housemother. She was a commanding personage, a widow, around fifty.

I suppose it's generally assumed—no doubt accurately in many cases—that a person who would want to devote his or her career to caring for poor, dear little blind children is motivated by compassion, selflessness, and social conscience. Less obvious is the possible motivation—perhaps residing in the same person—to control easy victims, per-

haps going so far as fulfilling a need to inflict cruelty under
the self-serving guise of doing good. One of the best-drawn
characters in modern literature to illustrate this all-too-
common syndrome among the so-called helping profes-
sions is the portrait of Nurse Ratched in *One Flew Over
the Cuckoo's Nest.*

I loved Mrs. Reinhold, in the same sense, I suppose,
that inmates at a death camp are said to become devoted to their guards. I was a scared babe and she was
authority. I grew up eager to please, and she cultivated
being pleased. And I must have sensed sharply and early
that the alternative to loving her was to have the daily
world of school and dorm turn suddenly harsh.

The first time I sensed the pervasive power of Mrs.
Reinhold was one day when her leathery voice suddenly
materialized in the boys' bathroom: "What's taking you so
long? Who's in that stall over there? Is some pig in there
jiggling?"

I had not heard that word with that implication before,
nor have I since, but at our refined school for blind children
the word "jiggling" was constantly in the air, laden with
fascinating, ominous, forbidden meanings. It was Mrs.
Reinhold's unique contribution to the language.

Although I was not the accused one in the stall, her
stunning indictment filled me with instant fear and guilt. I
was sure she knew—and was stripping my secret for everyone to see—that in the past year or two I had discovered
the wicked delight of lying naked on my bed (at home,
never at Overbrook, heaven forbid), rubbing myself against
my warm, surprisingly friendly foam pillow. One day my
mother caught me and her "David, what are you doing?"
confirmed that I was doing something very, very wrong.
I don't know if I'd ever heard the rumor that I would grow
hair on my palm, and certainly not that if I did it too much
I'd go blind, but I did come to believe that any time I did
it, the next day would be horrible. And sure enough, some-

thing bad would always happen next day. I did it a lot, and bad things kept happening a lot. What further proof would a perceptive young man need?

Mrs. Reinhold *knows!* I could not have felt more exposed. Mrs. Reinhold slept in a room at the end of our dorm, and for privacy during the night she required no more than the closing of a screen door at her entrance. Which didn't do much for *our* privacy. Dawn was often heralded by her bellowed announcement: "I didn't get a bit of sleep because of *this* big *pig*." Sometimes I knew whom she was singling out, sometimes I didn't. "He just jiggled and shook his bed all night." It never occurred to me then to wonder how come she heard so much so keenly from a distance when I, sharing the offender's room, didn't hear a thing.

Keeping the good opinion of Mrs. Reinhold increasingly became a matter of fearful urgency. After she'd accuse a boy of jiggling, others would start taunting him as a jiggler. Not as teasing, but in earnest. More threatening still, boys appointed themselves vigilantes to nail offenders whom Mrs. Reinhold had not yet got around to accusing. Time began taking the form of a race. Could I elude being accused—and disgraced beyond what my imagination could cope with—until I earned the status of one of her enforcers?

I made it. In the seventh grade I became one of her older boys charged with disciplining the younger, less domesticated ones. I felt I'd arrived on the day she first said, "Hartman, someone's been jiggling in the bathtub. I want you to get him and make sure he gets a cold bath." Often she was not satisfied to delegate responsibility. She'd burst into the bath chamber, select a culprit, and administer the cold bath herself.

Mrs. Reinhold and her zeal for moral purity were probably responsible for my troubles with that nasty little squirt who liked to sneak-punch me in the halls. I knew—

everybody knew—him to be a fervent jiggler. One day at gym, concerned for his destiny, I asked, "Why do you jiggle?"

" 'Cause I like it."

"You're screwing up your whole life."

"Why? How can it hurt me?"

I scarcely knew where to begin. How do you handle the ignorance of a sixth-grader? Although I was in seventh I didn't know specifically what to tell him, having a general sense, but not the precise proof, that it would make you into a rapist or something. So I said as knowledgeably as I could, "It's going to screw up your sexual relations with women later." He remained unpersuaded and decided to fix me good for being Mrs. Reinhold's trained pet.

In seventh grade—my third year of knowing Mrs. Reinhold—a startling realization hit me: I didn't love that housemother at all. I faced the truth squarely: I hated her.

Today I have a lingering, apparently ineradicable suspicion of people who cloak their lives in doing good, submerging their troubled identities "unselfishly" in social projects and institutionalized compassion. In the world of "helping" the blind, as well as in other "helping" worlds, doing good is not uncommonly a cover for exploiting the helpless and the pitied by establishing superiority and control over them. Whenever I sniff one of those helpful busybodies, I can't help but see such "devotion" in its ultimate, grotesque form, my mind drifting to dear, lovable, concerned Mrs. Reinhold, whose whole being was devoted to protecting us from ourselves.

For all my spinning of horror tales, I'm grateful to Overbrook and for the four years I spent there. One incomparable experience it gave me—which I was never to have again throughout public school, college, and medical training—was the privilege of equality, total acceptance, being treated like everybody else. Being blind didn't make me special, I didn't have to cope with anybody's pity. I think I'd rather deal with cruelty than pity. Being a victim of cruelty at least enables me, if I so choose, to feel superior to the person who's trying to inflict his superiority on me.

Overbrook taught me, as no ordinary school could, basic skills of living blind in a sighted world. I learned how a blind person washes, dresses, packs a suitcase, avoids losing possessions or leaving them behind. I learned to read in Braille. I had an occasional teacher who was inspiring and great—and who can count more than one, two, at most three mind-stretching teachers in a school career?

I can't quite put my finger on what there was about the attitude of my fifth-grade teacher, Dave Rudolph, that lit up my life. I'll just settle for recalling that one day he brought in chunks of balsa wood and a collection of sharp wood-carving knives. The flirtation with danger was thrilling. The fact is no one cut off his finger or bled to death, though there were a few nicks, and I can't think of a better way to learn that a knife is sharp. He also brought a collection of carved models we could feel and copy. I chose a dog. Mr. Rudolph would slice a groove out of the top of the block, say, and another groove on the side, and he'd instruct, "Now cut out all the wood between those two lines." By God, it came out a dog. I still have it and prize it. At the end of the project he gave out a prize for carving, and I got it. I think that's because I was his pet to begin with. And he was my favorite, partly because his name was Dave, too.

Then there was our Boy Scout troop, which helped prepare me for regular Boy Scouts later. And Overbrook and Mr. Chelli introduced me to wrestling, which was to play an important part in my school life and personal development in the coming years.

One part of my life that did not totally change when I lost my sight revolved around church and Sunday school.

We had a youth fellowship that met every Sunday night and often socialized on Friday night, doing things that bordered on the sinful, like playing spin the bottle. In my sixth grade at Overbrook the fellowship elected me president, the most exciting thing imaginable. I suspect the members felt it might be chic to have a blind leader. Whatever their reason, I was immensely flattered. I loved chairing those meetings, except the night I dropped my gavel and, leaning over to pick it up, I slammed my mouth on the lectern. The skin of my lip split and blood spurted all over everything. Members were horrified and I was mortified. I felt like that blind idiot I so dreaded being.

I envied Bobbie every Monday morning for being able to stay home with my parents all week, always feeling I was denied something precious. I don't recall ever imploring my parents to please let me go to regular school. It just got to be a family assumption that it would be good for me.

The prospect was exhilarating, not just because it meant staying home, being a seven-day part of my family, but for symbolic reasons that have only recently come clear. I'm not sure I ever totally got rid of that childish third-grade idea that through will and prayer I could get my sight back —an idea tied to leaving Overbrook. Four years later I think the prospect of leaving Overbrook somehow suggested a return to normality, that somehow I was no longer as blind as I once was.

✂ 6 ✂

Into the World
of the Sighted

Entering junior high in the public school system not only enlarged my vision of the world but, more literally, enlarged my world's physical scale. The small buildings at Overbrook had corridors just about wide enough for two peope to pass one another. Moving down a hallway you were always braced to bump into somebody. If you did, one of you stepped to the side and fingered your way along the opposite wall, thinking nothing of it. But at Haverford, a public junior high, the walls were a mile apart. It was frightening to give up the security of a wall. You could get lost before finding the opposite one, and if another corridor intersected where you were looking, you could grope and wander till hell-and-gone, never finding it.

Remember, for me this was a move from a twelve-grade school of 350 to a three-grade junior high of perhaps 1800; from a seventh grade of 20 students to an eighth grade of 600; from classroom groups of 11 to throngs of 30. Most disorienting of all, from a small school where everyone was blind to a large one where I was unique for probing my way around with a white cane.

The experience was new not only for me but for every-

one else. The kids at Haverford generally tried to be nice
to me, helping me from class to class, but they didn't always
know how to, or were too shy to, or were afraid I might
be embarrassed to accept their help. I hated to bump into
people. Whereas at Overbrook it didn't mean a thing, here
it embarrassed others and therefore embarrassed me because
that was not the way I wanted to become well known. So
once in the right room—and often I couldn't be totally
sure it was—I had to learn to find my chair coolly and
gracefully with a minimum of bumping. Finally seated, I
was free to let my mind range on the most compelling subject of the new experience: wondering who the girls were
on either side. Scary as the big classes and big school were,
the compensating advantage was that the more people, the
more girls.

The new blind kid was upsetting and puzzling to teachers, just as they were to him. I simply assumed that students
and teachers developed relationships in the same personal
way we did at Overbrook. After one of my first science
classes I thought it an obligation, since I'd usually won the
science prizes at Overbrook, to inform my science teacher
that I was particularly interested in science and would like
to do special projects. He said hesitantly, "Well, that's
fine." Maybe he thought I wanted special help because I
couldn't see the color in a test tube or see an amoeba
through a microscope. And maybe he felt unequipped to
offer whatever it was he imagined I was asking for. I just
know he didn't then, or any time later, suggest a special
project. That was my first experience with what has since
become a common, almost daily rediscovery of how uneasy, awkward, even frightened, otherwise commanding
personalities often become in the unfamiliar territory of
dealing with someone who can't see.

The new school made me suddenly aware, as I never was
before, of my blindness. It gave me an urgent need, a crav-
ing, for straightforward, reliable feedback from the im-

mediate environment. I wanted to be able to look into a mirror and say, "I look okay." I wanted to be able to check people's faces, their eyes, double-check that their reaction to something I said was what I thought it was.

Not long after starting public school I was fitted with scleral lenses, more simply called "caps." They're plastic covers over the eyeballs, decorated with fake irises, making them look like honest-to-goodness eyes, pupils and all. One reason I needed them was that the surface of my eye occasionally accumulated specks of calcium that irritated the delicate inside of the eyelid. But chiefly they're cosmetic, so effectively that they sometimes make people unaware that the wearer is blind. The caps are popped in and out about as easily as contact lenses. I've been told I have a slight tendency to aim the direction of my "looking" at people not quite at their eyes but somewhere in the middle of their foreheads, like staring at Cyclops. So I try to focus on their nostrils—just above their voices—hoping to hit them right in the eyeballs.

I guess I was never fully convinced of the magic of the caps until the opening days of my junior year of high school when I raised my hand to ask a question of my new physics teacher. "Let me describe it to you," she replied and started drawing a picture on the board. I'll ride along with that, I figured, knowing that sometimes teachers draw for their own clarity of mind before verbally launching into their answer. Then she asked, "In that case, which way would the arrow be pointing?" Aha, the Socratic method. Throw the question back at the student and let him do the thinking. I replied, "Sorry, but I can't see what you're doing." I was sitting right in the first row. She laughed apologetically, erased her drawing, and drew it again—presumably more artistically.

"Now which way?"

I decided to be blunt: "I really can't tell you. I can't see it at all."

She laughed. The class laughed even louder, I couldn't tell whether at me, at her, or at the failure of communication. I momentarily enjoyed the attention.

"Okay," she surrendered good-naturedly, not wanting on the first day of school to alienate either smartass me or the class. She proceeded to hand out books. The guy next to me whispered, "Dave, she still doesn't get it."

"For the fifteen minutes remaining in the hour," the teacher resumed, "I want you all to read Chapter One."

After a few minutes of just sitting there, I decided to rest, putting my head down. I had acquired a Braille copy of our textbook, but, not expecting to need it today, had left it home. The teacher, her patience thinning, said, "Hartman, you're not reading."

I replied, "I'm not kidding, I can't see."

With finality, she hurled back the classic teacher response: "Well, why don't you get glasses?"

The point of all this is that those caps are pretty convincing.

For all those bumps along the road, the transition to public school was happy and liberating. And while I have most of my teachers and fellow students to thank, I would single out one individual more than any other, Millie Landis, the school system's itinerant teacher for handicapped students.

I adored Mrs. Landis as much for her warmth and friendliness as for her ingenuity at helping me reduce overwhelming problems to simple ones. She'd make sure I saw my new teachers in advance of each semester, find out what textbooks I'd need so there'd be plenty of time to order Braille copies, which often had to be specially made by the Volunteer Service for the Blind in downtown Philadelphia or sent to New York to be taped by Recordings for the Blind. Whenever I sensed a special problem with a teacher who might feel uneasy with a blind student, Mrs. Landis would bring us together to work out methods that would be comfortable for both teacher and student. Sometimes she'd administer tests to me. That meant reading me the questions, which often a regular teacher couldn't find time to do or was too uneasy to do. Sometimes all sorts of anxieties, academic or social or whatever, would build up, and she'd help me break it down to particulars, isolate what was really bothering me, saying, "Let's look at this and work this problem out."

In short, Mrs. Landis taught me confidence—that a big, vague glob of emotional turmoil can be reduced to specifics; that something can be done about almost anything; that any person, even a blind person, can manage his environment enough to claim a guiding control over the course of his life. I came to believe that there is rarely an excuse for any person to feel like a helpless cork on a rolling sea, even though many people live all the days of their lives feeling that way.

In tenth grade or so I got upset over school dances. I'd attend them but would just stand there and not do anything. How would I ask a girl to dance, or be asked by her? Mrs. Landis would say, "All right, let's think about how to deal with this," and we'd figure out places to stand where I'd be most likely to get into conversation and appear available, or ways to ask other guys to introduce me to some of the girls. And finally, the problem of dancing itself. I danced awkwardly. Some basic dance movements are hard to explain to a blind person. Sighted learners have the advantage of mirrored walls in a dance studio, so if they're prancing like camels they can see how bad they look. Mrs. Landis and I figured out that I needed individualized instruction by a patient, sympathetic, verbally skilled dancing teacher, and she helped find one at the Mary Downey dancing school.

If Millie Landis was the best teacher in my life, the worst was one of my teachers of German, Herr Volkenberg. (He made us say "Herr," but Volkenberg is made up.) I slowly learned to hate him as it gradually dawned on me that he hated me from the first moment he saw me. I have to believe he hated me for my blindness. He hated anything that was not perfect. Herr Volkenberg informed me right off that it was going to be tough for a blind student to learn German, which made no sense to me but I thought I'd wait and see. When the Braille edition of my German book was a week late in arriving he implied that I was trying to duck out of work.

For my first test I studied hard and went through it cold. (Hatred can be a marvelous motivator.) When the results came out, however, my paper was marked with a 60, a failing grade. I couldn't believe it. It turned out that thirty out of the forty lost points were for a list of words I had to supply in plural, an instruction that was not given to me. When I found that out, I looked for the student whom Herr Volkenberg had appointed to administer the exam to me. She promptly went to him, pleading, "It was my fault. I didn't read him the part about making them plural. He shouldn't lose that score."

Herr Volkenberg looked down the list, and all my words were correct, except that they were in singular. Grudgingly he muttered, "Oh, I see," and raised my score to a 90. He was so bugged by having to give me those thirty points back that the next day in class he brought up the matter of plurals, taunting, "Some of us here have trouble with plurals, haven't they, Hartman? You want to give us some plurals, Hartman?" He made me stand up, and kept working me over like that in front of everybody.

Another time he ordered me to start reading from a certain page in the textbook. The pages of my Braille book, of course, are numbered differently and I had to fuss around finding the correct passage. "Herr Hartman," he snarled, "you're not trying to use your blindness as a crutch, are you now? We don't want people here spending their time feeling sorry for themselves. We've all got to pick up our load and carry it."

I wanted to murder him.

The next day my father took a half-day off from work to visit Herr Volkenberg. Dad began by saying he was sure that Germany had some blind people and that surely they had learned the language, and he didn't see why his son, who was doing extremely well in everything else— mostly A's and only a few B's—couldn't take a course in this public school in German on the same terms as every- body else. Herr Volkenberg rose as though to walk out, but Dad startled him with a command: "You sit down! We came here to settle something." The Prussian bully meekly obeyed, whimpering something about not seeing how a blind person could learn German.

Dad cowed Herr Volkenberg into making feeble little promises to treat me the same as others, but we knew he was unchangeable. Fortunately (for me), the following year he was no longer at my school.

In biology I qualified by the skin of my teeth for the "academically talented" class, and, having become increas- ingly turned on over the years about a medical career, this special privilege greatly excited me. I still remember vividly the first day in that class, running down the agenda of the year's work, being thrilled at the sounds of the mysterious worlds we would soon enter: cytology, the study of cells; histology, the study of tissues; genetics, the study of genes. I took furious notes on my Braille puncher, and at home that night felt heady, confident—overconfident. The next day we had a quiz. I flunked. I hadn't bothered to study.

It was like the end of the world. My hopes of staying in the academically talented group—my whole career— had just gone down the drain because of a couple of hours of laziness. Devastated, I approached my teacher to explain my foolish neglect. All he said was, "I'm sure you're going to do well. Just relax and don't worry."

I did relax—somewhat—as I tried to engrave in my head that I, of all people, just couldn't afford the luxury of let-

ting up for even a day if I wanted to avoid being drowned
in the onrush of schoolwork. Some other bright kid could
do it now and then and make it up by cramming, but even
trying to cram took me twice, three times as long. Goofing
off was an option I just didn't have.

My across-the-yard neighbor Don Jarvis and I found
we were both peculiarly magnetized by biology. We spun
fantasies of organizing the whole biological world, classi-
fying every known type of animal into some scheme of
genetic organization. Don did his drawings and classifica-
tions with pencil and paper, I with my raised-line drawing
kit. The truth soon crept over us that this was a task of
impressive dimension and that its completion might have
to be put off for a while—at least beyond our tenure in
ninth grade.

In my junior year of high school a lot of my friends
asked, "Why don't you run for president of the student
council?" Flattery is flattery, so I ran. Out of four candidates, I came in first, which qualified me to run in a two-
candidate runoff. Each of the two finalists had to make a
speech at school assembly. As front-runner, I felt very
presidential and delivered an oration heavily weighted with
responsibility and wisdom: the importance of working har-
moniously with the faculty, of not being too demanding
or obnoxious. I tremble today to think how terrible it was.
My opponent said, "I'm going to give you this, give you
that, we're going to fight to win our [unspecified] cause."
In the vote he clobbered me. As loser, I became vice-president, pledging silently to retire forever from politics.

The most compelling and consuming of all high-school
subjects, of course, is making a hit with girls (or boys, as
the case may be). But I can't properly relate how I did
that without first telling about my affair with varsity
wrestling—which was how I made my hit with girls.

At Overbrook I had been wrestling since third grade. It was more or less required in gym because wrestling is one of the few sports blind kids can engage in without greatly modifying the rules. We had Mighty Mite tournaments for kids from third to sixth grades. Every year in my first match I'd be pitted against some terrified, muscleless jellyfish and I'd beat him. Then, because I was pudgy, they'd pair me against someone equal to my weight who was usually older, and not pudgy, all muscle. That guy would come at me—*whaaam!*—and pin me right away. Finally I got to sixth grade, the last year you could be a Mighty Mite. All those older guys had gone on to seventh grade or higher, so I was king.

The upshot was that now, entering junior high in public school, I had experience in wrestling. I knew the tricks of the mat better than these sighted guys. My sister Bobbie spurred me with an offer to pay for half of a $20 varsity sweater if I earned the right to wear it.

I had another slight advantage over sighted kids in wrestling. They weren't sure how to deal with me. My opponent and I would go out to the middle of the mat, face each other off, the whistle would blow, and I could just hear his hesitation: Gosh, if it's not fair to hit a kid with glasses, what do you do with a guy who can't see at all? In that split second, he was all mine. *Wham!* I'd lunge at him and take him down. He'd be shocked, then embarrassed that the coach and all his teammates and maybe some girls watching from the walls of the gym were all seeing this blind kid beat the hell out of him, and finally he'd get mad. By that time I was on top, working him over. When you're that close, it's all feel. Seeing doesn't help.

I remember my first match against Upper Darby, our big rival school. I pinned my opponent in forty-five seconds. That's very fast—a match usually lasts six minutes. This guy didn't hesitate. He brought me down first. As I toppled, he slamming on top of me, instinctively one of my arms wrapped around his head; the other grabbed at his leg. In that instant I remembered something I learned—or something another guy didn't learn—at Overbrook.

That Overbrook opponent was bigger than me and quicker. He'd grab my head in one arm, my leg in another, pull them together till I almost tore in two. I couldn't breathe. I'd want to scream. Yet through my agony I'd be elated. To beat a guy by pinning him, you've got to press both his shoulders flat to the ground and hold them there for a count of three. As long as this guy kept trying to tear my head out of my neck, he was doing the opposite of pinning me. I wanted to scream at him, "You damn fool! Roll over me, loosen that headhold and press my shoulders to the mat!" The fool never did.

Now, having grabbed this Upper Darby guy's head and leg, with one stunning yank I squeezed them together until he could stick his own knee in his eye, then rolled my body toward his head as though to mash him into a pancake. And that was it. The match was over. My first big pin.

To pin a guy in the first two-minute period of a three-period match is like being God. Power. Control. You're not only on top of your opponent, you're on top of the world. And, Upper Darby being our rival, the whole gym was packed. All those people watching, admiring. Look at that blind guy! He crippled that brute from Upper Darby. It still stands as the biggest thrill of my life.

Actually, through my six years of junior high and high school, I was not the wrestling superstar I dreamed of being. Eventually other wrestlers learned that even when your opponent is blind you have to exploit every weakness. So if I learned in that first year or two how to psych them out, they soon learned how to psych me out. My six-year record of wins and losses wound up fair to middling, but I did make the varsity every year but one and enjoyed wearing that sweater that Bobbie half-bought for me.

✂✂ 7 ✂✂

Blind Dating

The most disconcerting, yet delightful, change upon entering junior high from Overbrook was the easy association with girls. At Overbrook the main rule about boys and girls playing together had been that they mustn't. Play areas were segregated. The people who ran Overbrook believed that blind people must not become tempted to marry other blind people.

And a temptation it is. After the comfortable, accepting atmosphere of a school for the blind, a young person has a deep urge to avoid the threats of sighted society—to take refuge in mating with someone who shares the inability to see. But often experiences of the blind marrying the blind have turned out impractical. If two people with different handicaps marry—say, blind with deaf, or blind with lame—there's no reason they would not have a normal chance at an excellent marriage, one partner providing the eyes for both, the other providing the ears or the limbs. I share Overbrook's feeling that the blind should not be encouraged to marry the blind. My objection is only to their preposterous means of trying to make boys pretend there's no such thing as girls, and vice versa.

During segregated recess at Overbrook, boys whispered and absorbed more wondrous and forbidden secrets about girls than they ever would have gleaned if girls were nearby. Partially sighted guys who had seen their mothers and sisters naked, or their brothers' or fathers' bawdy magazines, would tell others of the marvels they had secretly come upon. And the jokes they told, while not always funny, often startled. We third-, fourth-, and fifth-graders didn't have much to contribute, but we worked hard at concealing our eagerness not to miss a syllable of the swaggering wisdom of the sixth- and seventh-graders.

One older student, a black guy named Alex, took a big-brother interest in me, but in protecting me from the pitfalls that might be opened by the dangerous talk of his peers, he himself revealed some pretty bewildering secrets. He said that sometimes males made advances toward other males, and he urged that this vice be withstood at all costs. If awakened from a slumber by a homosexual's stimulation, Alex confided to me, "even a priest" couldn't resist the ecstasy of it. The impression he made was deep.

Not that I had come to these schoolyard seminars entirely devoid of knowledge; I had once quizzed my father about the secrets of sex and actually found that I knew more than he did.

"Dad, how does a lady get pregnant?" I was seven years old, not yet blinded. Dad had just come home from work and scarcely had his coat off. Thinking seriously and long about my question, he finally announced:

"God makes the woman pregnant."

"Then how come the baby gets born looking like both the mother and father?"

Another long pause. "Well, when two people get married, God crosses their strings in the sky and that makes the mother pregnant. That's why the baby looks like the father and the mother, because of those strings."

"How come some women get pregnant when they're not married?"

Dad's manner and voice told me he was moving onto uncertain ground. "Well, now, I guess God does make mistakes."

"Ellen got pregnant. How come Ellen is so ashamed if it was God's mistake, not hers?"

"Who's Ellen?"

"You know, *Ellen*. On 'As the World Turns.'"

Dad had no answer for me. He muttered, "I didn't see it, so I can't tell you."

One night soon after I returned from Boston sightless, Dad was out playing poker and Mom must have decided it was time for me to have that little talk that she knew Dad intended one day to give me but would keep putting off. She started a vague conversation with me about babies and how they get there. I don't think I learned much, but it was a terrible ordeal for Mom. Years later she told me she got through it only because she knew I couldn't look her in the eye, and therefore she didn't have to look straight at me.

The truth is, I didn't launch my sex life until years later. Three years later, actually. In the sixth grade I fell in love for the first time. Her name was Helaine. I can't explain why Helaine set me on fire. She wasn't my type. From bumping into her in the hall I knew that her arm had almost the circumference of my thigh. But she had champagne bubbles in her laugh, and that laugh seeped all through her voice. Furthermore, she had the high-status attribute of being able to see a little. She took to guiding me around the halls, the best part of which was that she had to take my hand.

Teachers soon stopped that, but just off an Overbrook corridor there was an alcove not readily visible to teachers, and you could hear footsteps of anyone approaching. This place was called the Kissing Corner in honor of the wicked, forbidden things that went on there. The most exciting contest at Overbrook was a boy and girl seeing how many times they could kiss in the Kissing Corner before footsteps forced them to flee in opposite directions, each of them the picture of innocence.

Helaine tantalized me with tales of the Kissing Corner, and we decided that right after Christmas we'd bite the apple ourselves. I couldn't wait to get home to tell Mom and Dad and Bobbie about—well, not exactly about our plan, but at least about Helaine and the existence of the Kissing Corner.

"You wouldn't kiss Helaine there, would you?" Mom inquired apprehensively.

"Oh, I'd never do that," I hastily assured her, not knowing to this day whether Mom was worried that I'd break a school rule, or worried that I'd be stirred by Helaine's passion into the life of a hedonist, or whether Mom was just kidding. But having promised Mom, I considered myself barred from doing it.

Telling Helaine after Christmas of my promise didn't do much for our relationship. While still reserving a fond spot, albeit a scarred one, for me, Helaine took up with an older guy, about fifteen, who entertained her with a line of talk I could never match. He claimed (so she told me) that he used to violate his cousin. A housemother stumbled on a packet of letters between this rake and Helaine in which they had scrawled in oversized script some plans for an all-the-way tryst of their own. The guy was kicked out of Overbrook, and Helaine was suspended. I didn't see how ejection would prevent them from sinning, but at least it prevented them from sinning at Overbrook. For a long time I felt somewhat responsible for Helaine's fall from grace. Our plan for a limited experiment in the Kissing Corner might have saved her from getting involved with that man who dragged her down the garden path.

I was ripe for a rebound affair, and it came in the person of Ramona. I'd had my eye on Ramona even while otherwise engaged with Helaine. Ramona was short and petite, traits that appeal to me. Also, very pretty—sighted guys assured me of that, and it felt then (as it still does today) important to get that assurance. Our sixth-grade teacher assigned everyone in class to write a short play by the following week, the best play to be produced before the class. I won the competition because I was the only one who turned in a script. The others just couldn't face the creative agony. My play was about a king and queen visiting a quaint town in their domain, and how a lovable but laughable donkey messed up the royal visit. Over Ramona's protests, I cast her as the donkey. Like most sixth-grade lovers, I confused taunting with flirting: Just be beastly to her and she'll notice you. It wasn't until seventh grade that I realized girls like boys to be nice to them. So goodbye, Ramona.

Heartbreaking as those minor episodes were, I didn't know what suffering was until the summer following my first year of junior high—and Estelle. I was visiting another brother of my mother's, Uncle Hoppy, at his home on the New Jersey shore, a visit I always made eagerly. Estelle, a fellow student at Haverford, where she was very popular, was summering there in the same seaside town. After a few days on the beach, I made the bold move of asking if she'd spend the evening with me doing the rides at the amusement park. She accepted!

Early in the evening, munching a highly spiced pizza, we strolled down the boardwalk. Boardwalk strolling was nice. She could hold onto my arm, making me feel very manly, and at the same time guide me. She was good at it. As we approached a clamor of merry, scared cries, Estelle exclaimed, "That looks like a fun ride!" The riders, she explained excitedly, sat in pairs in little cars that hung loosely from an enormous rotating wheel. They swung back and forth, this way and that, chaotically, while the wheel churned them up and over and down. Judging by the screams, it seemed an adventure, all right.

It was. No sooner had we achieved full speed and full

tilt when, not being able to see, I became totally disoriented. I couldn't tell up from down. One instant, plummeting; the next, weightless. The peppery pizza! While I was going down, it was coming up. I was going to barf all over the amusement park—all over Estelle! I reswallowed that pizza over and over, anything to avoid ruining Estelle's impression of me. I was overwhelmed by a suddenly realized rule of life: It is not masculine to vomit on your girl friend.

Though I managed to contain myself and the pizza, the evening was a disaster. Despite that, I hoped for some sign later in the week that Estelle still liked me, and in fact when I saw her on the beach she was jolly and friendly. But the sparks of my fantasy of a romance with Estelle did not erupt into a blaze. (Over the years I've loosely kept in touch with Estelle. She went through medical school about the same time I did and has become a physician.)

Before long I became something of a hero at Haverford. Or at least a curio. I was that blind guy with a wrestling record of six wins against only one loss, and a good pinner of my opponents. For the first time in memory, Haverford students, and even students from other schools, were turning out to watch wrestling—and me. Someone passed the word that a stunning cheerleader named Vicki wanted to meet me. Coating my uncontainable eagerness with all the cool I could muster, I waved a nonchalant hand and said, "Sure."

Our go-between introduced us in a hallway. I liked the music in Vicki's voice. I liked the clear melody of her being impressed with me. I liked her being short. I almost went out of my mind every night for the rest of the week wondering what to do about her. Finally, Dad prodded, "Instead of worrying to *us* constantly about her, why don't you ask her out?" Getting Vicki on the phone, I suggested with the suavity of one who's been doing this every week in his life, "Why don't we go to a movie this Friday night. My dad will drive." Whoops, that was a slip, but then I remembered that a lot of kids in our set, too young for licenses, depended upon parents to drive them on dates.

She seemed eager. I couldn't believe it.

As Friday night crept toward me with agonizing lethargy, I plotted my moves. I would not—absolutely would not—have Dad walk me to her door and stand there while she greeted me. Horrors. But how *would* I work it? I arranged with Dad that he'd bring me up her long walk, then he'd run back to the car and slam the car door so I'd hear it, then I'd ring the bell and there I'd be, in all my self-sufficient splendor.

It worked out well, and the movie must have been good because I don't remember that it was bad. Dad had returned and was waiting for us out front. Vicki and I slipped into the back seat and I put my arm around her shoulders, outwardly just as confident and composed as can be, inwardly expecting momentarily her searing scream and flight from the car. To my surprise she snuggled into my armpit and kept on talking about the movie, happily, sort of affectionately, as though what I'd done was perfectly natural. How could this wonderful thing be happening to me? A *cheerleader*. When the car pulled up to her house, like any man about town I got out with her to escort her to the door, aware, terrified, that it was going to be damn tough getting back to the car. But I was going to work it out some way. Dad was *not* going to walk us to the door.

At the door, incredibly, she seemed to wait a meaningful moment. I committed myself to the risk—I kissed her goodnight. To this day I have no idea what I hit. Either she had turned her head, or she had a beard. I'm still puzzled.

Beard or not, next day I was giddy with visions of going steady with Vicki. By the following Wednesday I collected enough nerve to call her again.

"I can't go out Friday," she regretted. "I have to baby-sit my kid brother. But you can come over."

Unbelievable! My fantasies were somewhat scary because at fifteen I held firm ideas about celibacy before marriage, but surely she was sending me an undisguised invitation to the blurry, enthralling high-school world of deep-kissing, which was known in the Haverford crowd as "making out."

The first inkling of disaster came when I arrived at her door. Some other girl was there. I guess I shouldn't have been miffed over two for the price of one, but she could have mentioned on the phone that a friend was dropping by. Then, before long, came a knock at the door, and in sauntered some creepy guy whom Vicki introduced as her boy friend.

I knew the guy. Sort of. I knew enough about him to know I didn't want to know him. He never went out for sports, but every day carried a different book about weight lifting. He'd flunked a grade, was always getting suspended, and eventually was kicked out of school. In every way, I perceived him as inferior to me. How could Vicki choose *him?* I felt had, humiliated, unmanned, and he made matters unbearably worse by not seeming at all concerned about my presence. They went right ahead and talked about a school dance, their dating plans, and whatnot, making me feel like an eavesdropper and even less.

Why had she told a mutual friend she wanted to meet me? Just to satisfy a curiosity? Instead of paying her way into a freak show, did she want the freak show—the blind wrestler—to come to her, the cheerleader? Why did she lead me into having this painful crush on her, which I now had to endure and get rid of all by myself? What had I done, or not done, to leave her so obviously untouched? What gave this guy the confidence that I was not even a potential threat?

It was one of those moments—and they have recurred since—when I found myself strangely grateful that I was blind. My blindness had to be the reason she was treating me like an unfeeling thing, like dirt, like nothing. If it couldn't be blamed on that, it had to be blamed on *me*. And that would have been unbearable.

At the end of the torturous evening, Vicki, holding my hand in both of hers, cooed, "Dave, I *do* want to be friends with you. Let's *do* things together." And dope that I was, I took that as a sign of hope. Maybe if she just got to know me . . . A friend of mine was going with a friend of hers, so once or twice in pairs we took walks around her neighborhood, she holding my arm or holding hands. I wanted her. Well, I'm not sure it was *her* I wanted, but I fiercely wanted to break into the school social crowd and she was very high up on the list socially. If she started liking me I'd go to the best parties and everything that went with it.

But I didn't make it.

All this time, all during my eighth-grade year, Helaine kept calling me from Overbrook. It was difficult to resist the temptation of pursuing that. I ached to be liked, and Helaine clearly liked me. But I ached even more to prove that I could succeed socially in the public school. I kept hearing the taunting I-told-you-so voice of Mrs. Reinhold. A guy I knew from Overbrook had left for public school, and when he came back to visit Overbrook, Mrs. Reinhold needled him: "I bet you wish you were back here again among your own." Something cracked in him—she'd hit her target, and in a few weeks he was back. Later, he tried to explain to me. "Kids out there don't treat you as well as they do here. Overbrook is better." What he meant was that it's more comfortable to be king among the blind than a competitor with a handicap in the real world.

I won't put him down for preferring that satisfaction, but I didn't want it. I wanted to make it in public high school, in the world of everybody. If I couldn't make it with Vicki, I'd find someone to make it with. But Helaine symbolized a temptation I had to refuse.

Permit one more horror story, a ninth-grade one: Joyce.

Joyce was going with Eddie McConnal, a fellow wrestler. He was a good friend and teammate, except that he was always going to those great parties to which I was never invited, and I kept wishing that someday he'd help me get in with the crowd. Joyce and Eddie broke up just before a big school dance, and Joyce made no secret of the fact that she was brokenhearted and soul-crushed. Seizing the opportunity (under the guise of sympathy) I said, "I'll take you."

Word of my love reached our young wrestling coach, Dale Bonsall, who was a big brother, almost a father, to many guys at school, and whom I just worshiped. "Listen," the coach urged me, "drop this dame. She's no good for you. She'll hurt you. Don't take her. Promise me that, and someday I'll set you up with an airline stewardess." I didn't see how I could get out of it, and I guess I didn't really want to. Joyce was pretty hot stuff.

Between the time of my invitation and the night of the dance, I heard that Eddie and Joyce had made up, but that didn't bother me as I showed up at her door excitedly, corsage in hand. At the dance she kept saying she had to go to the bathroom and would disappear for long periods, leaving me to keep silent company with a wall.

I'm not sure whether I allowed it to occur to me then, or whether I thought of it later, but I suspected that Eddie had come with or without another girl, that they were meeting somewhere, maybe even dancing, and that I was being used to fill the spaces in her time.

The worst came at a party afterward, one of those "in" parties that I'd been so eager to attend. It was small, subdued, about five couples and a layout of awfully good food. I was sitting in a tall, hardbacked chair, next to Joyce, when gradually the subdued tone turned to conspicuous silence. Joyce whispered in my ear mischievously, "You know what everybody else is doing?" Everyone else was making out—which, I emphasize, in Haverford meant something short of earnest petting—and here I was sitting like a parson. Her whisper to me was unmistakably an invitation. Quelling my instant excitement and nervousness, I slipped an arm around her.

"Oops," she ooped coyly, "got to get something to eat." And she vanished from her chair.

I was positive that everyone was staring at me and my empty arm, suppressing uproarious laughter. I felt like a monstrous jackass, humiliated in front of this "in" group. I just wanted to collapse and cry. Or vanish through the floor. Or die. Or never show my face in that school again.

Over and over I told myself—and when I got home, over and over I told my parents—it's because I'm blind. I had to believe that.

Dating was hard work, requiring planning, attention to detail, persistence, and patience. If I met someone I thought might be interesting and if I learned, say, that we were going to have a class together the following semester, I'd start plotting how to arrange for our seats accidentally to be in proximity. I had to develop nonchalant ways of finding out what interesting girls were sitting around me, then figure out how to strike up conversations, each of which might take a day or two of planning. Before going too far, I'd always check with some guy I trusted: "Is she good-looking?" They'd usually give me straight answers.

Another planning problem was trying to figure out where and when certain desirable girls would pass by in the hallway so I could contrive to meet them there. Let's say between the fourth and fifth periods a certain girl I had my eye on had to turn a certain corner to get from her previous class to her next one. (One of the penalties of becoming interested in a girl was that I had to memorize her program.) I'd have to scoot out of my fourth-period class as quickly as I could and cane my way along a hallway wall with dispatch so I could just happen to be standing at that corner when she walked by. Then I'd just have to hope that she'd say, "Hi, Dave." If she said my name, I'd go bananas inside, have a small orgasm. I might respond with some carefully preplanned "spontaneous" comment, phrased to require another response from her, so I could walk a few yards beside her having an oh-so-casual conversation. Or sometimes I'd have to settle for just that "Hi, Dave," which was usually worth my effort.

If the oh-so-casual conversation reached the point where I could ask for a date, I'd prefer doing so on the telephone. On the phone, we were equals. I wouldn't have to worry about eye contact or whether she was in front of me or had silently moved beside me.

All through a date I'd worry as to whether I was aware of all the necessaries. Was my fly shut? I developed a slip-quick move in checking that, not knowing till much later that sighted guys are always doing the same thing. Another thing was remembering not to talk about anyone, especially girls, who might conceivably be nearby.

In short, dating was never a relaxed, enjoyable business, but a great labor to be worked at. Still, I was determined to succeed. I was always worried about the last date, planning ways to refine this or that on the next one. I've often said to Cheri that until we were married I never appreciated girls. All of a sudden I was free at last to relax and just make friends.

My family helped get me through this time of adolescent groping and suffering and learning. As always, my parents propped me up in one direction and Bobbie reliably pushed the opposite way. Whenever a girl said no to a date, regardless of her excuse I always assumed it was because she was ill at ease with blindness or uninterested in a blind guy. I'd feel put down, frustrated, helpless, angry. Mom would offer welcome sympathy: "That's a shame. Could we help you?" The sympathy alone would help. Dad was more direct and positive: "Call somebody else." As usual, Bobbie stepped in with unwanted, jarring realism: "You've got to remember, Dave, this happens to every guy. Every guy gets turned down for dates." Making matters worse, she'd add, "Lots of times I want a guy to call me for a date and he doesn't." That always hit me dramatically, because Bobbie was one of the more popular girls at school and I always envisioned her dating calendar as overflowing and trouble-free.

Bobbie's dashes of cold water against my parents' unreserved warm sympathy—and against my own self-pity—did me more good than I would ever have acknowledged at the time. For example, there was a girl I dated in Lansdale, about an hour's drive away. Mom or Dad would say, "Well, we'll drive you there," but Bobbie would jump in. "Dave, isn't there some way you can get there without putting Mom and Dad out?"

It was that old vacuum-cleaner hassle again, and I'd pout. My parents would get mad at her: "Bobbie, you should be more sensitive to Dave."

"He should be more sensitive to you. He's putting you out and maybe there's another way."

I have no illusion that Bobbie's only concern at the moment was to improve me or to protect Mom and Dad. I don't doubt that in some less-than-conscious way she was getting even for all the attention I got as a kid, often at her expense. But the results were positive all around. She did put me on the defensive, sensitizing me to an awareness that the world (personified by my parents) was not at my beck and call. I did have to exhaust the possible ways of helping myself before calling on others to help me. And at the same time, Bobbie raised Mom's and Dad's awareness that they (like all parents of blind kids) had a strong tendency to baby me, and that they had to guard against it. Neither I nor my parents have ever been sure of just why they resisted the lure of that overprotective route taken by most parents and thus avoided making an emotional cripple out of me. I am sure, however, that Bobbie had a lot to do with it.

While getting turned down by girls was frustrating, I was obstinate. One time I called through a list of eleven girls before finding a partner for a dance. The tension in the house would drive the family nuts. Mom couldn't down her meals, she'd be so fearful that each call would mean another failure for me.

One day Mom, knowing I was calling down a list of the most popular girls in school, asked in anguish, "Dave, why do you have to start at the top? Isn't there some nice, quiet little girl who'd love to have you ask her?"

Maybe there was. But how was I to know? Popular people usually are popular because they're outgoing. They talk easily to strangers, make their presence known. Those are the only ones whose existence I was likely to learn about. Sure, I might like some quiet jewel of a girl lingering alone in a quiet corner. But how would I know she was there? So I had no choice but to take on tough competition.

Besides, I did have this thing about not settling for less than I thought other guys would. Which, I suppose, accounts for my wanting other guys' assurance that a girl was pretty, by *their* standards. A fellow who had become my best friend, Wayne Hey, and I developed a simple number system for quick, disguised communication to me as to how a girl stacked up. We had a scale of zero to five. Someone I was about to meet (or had just met) got points for each of five characteristics: one point for attractive hair and face, and another each for superior boobs, hips, buttocks, and legs. The game made me feel very manly, but the truth, of course, is that I felt left out of what I assumed other boys knew about girls and their physiques.

One day in speech class I was assigned to debate on, of all things, pornography. I had to argue that it was evil and should be banned, a position I wasn't enthusiastic about, but that didn't stop me from putting the opportunity to good use. I convinced a friend—and my mother, whose sanction I felt for some reason I had to have—that I couldn't argue against pornography without knowing firsthand what I was against. My argument was so overpowering that this guy agreed to read all of *Fanny Hill* into a tape recorder for me. I was shocked and delighted at how vivid—and endlessly adventurous—that book is. Later I secretly re-recorded the hottest scenes on a single condensed tape and stashed it in a secret place exactly as most of my school-mates stashed a copy or two of girlie magazines. And for exactly the same reasons that they turned to their center-folds, I'd turn on *Fanny Hill* and let her turn me on as I went about doing what boys do.

During one of my high-school summers, Mom and Dad blew a good portion of their life savings to take Bobbie and me on a tour of Europe, which unexpectedly deepened my sex education. In the great museums, while the rest of the family admired classic paintings of nudes, I learned to ad-mire the statues. At first timidly, expecting other tourists to go berserk at the sight, I began feeling the statuary, lingering as long as I liked.

In Florence, so rich with the work of Michelangelo, in-cluding David (the original of which was mounted too high on a pedestal for me to explore), I discovered that I liked the forms of those perfect men as well as those of women. Then, as now, I was turned on by the structure of muscles. Maybe because muscles connote success in wrestling. Maybe because I had worked hard at developing my own, lifting weights and whatever. Maybe because I hadn't been taught by my sightless environment to repress the homosexuality that everyone is supposed to have some of and is expected to repress. All I know is I liked those statues.

Another memorable piece of learning that those museums provided was more anthropological than sexual. In the city that claims a copyright on romance, Paris, the museum guards rushed toward me like cops to a bank robbery the instant they saw me finger their precious marble boobs.

"*Non, non,*" they commanded. In Italy, by contrast, the guards rushed over, too, but as soon as they saw I couldn't see, they couldn't wait to take my hands and guide them over the best things to feel, afraid I might miss something. So much for which of your romance nations deserves the name.

✕✕ 8 ✕✕

Getting Hooked
on Medicine

In the back seat of a car on a Sunday night with the feeling outside of darkness and streetlights and families on the way home, it hit me like a shot out of nowhere: I wanted to be a doctor when I grew up.

Actually it was not exactly a shot out of nowhere. We had spent that Sunday on a happy visit to Uncle Chill, and I guess what my thought was really trying to say was that I wanted to grow up to be like—indeed, to *be*—Uncle Chill. Most of the time I thought of Uncle Chill more as an uncle than a doctor, but I vividly remembered one time when Chill doctored me in an emergency.

I was about seven, still able to see, visiting a sporting goods store with my dad, admiring a stand of fishing poles, when in my enthusiasm I jerked my hand downward, catching a fishhook in a finger. It stuck deeply, and to my horror it wouldn't come out. Dad scooped me into the car and ran me to Uncle Chill. What in the world would Chill do? I wondered. What *could* he do? The hook was designed to stay stuck in a fish no matter what, until the fish's face is torn up getting it out. Would he have to do that to my finger?

Uncle Chill looked at my wound and the protruding

hook calmly, knowledgeably. Then he picked up a funny-looking long pair of scissors—*What's he going to do?*—and simply pushed the hook end until it broke through the skin at another point, then snipped off the barb. Removing it painlessly, he then freely slid out the rest of the hook. How utterly bright! Uncle Chill is a genius! I would never have thought of that in a hundred years!

Seven years were to pass until that Sunday night on the way home when it first occurred to me that I might do what Uncle Chill does. I said nothing, either to Bobbie who was off in her own world at the opposite end of the back seat, or to my parents up front. This was important and had to be kept secret. I probably didn't announce it until sometime the next evening. At fourteen, I was able to keep secrets well, but not long.

One reason I kept it secret was that I suspected the thought would displease my father. Every once in a while we'd talk about what I might be when I became an adult, and I could tell it was an important and worrisome subject to Dad. More often than any other prospect, he'd mention my becoming a lawyer. Second, becoming a minister. But he never mentioned being a doctor. I wasn't sure he'd like it.

I remember once chatting with Uncle Chill about different kinds of doctors and what they do. In my inimitable way, I soon began talking about my idea at home—talking, talking, talking about it until my parents' ears were raw. My mother, limp with anxiety over the frustration her son was letting himself in for this time, decided that the cure was to be found at the source of the disease. Back we went to Uncle Chill.

"What do you think about this idea?" she asked, making sure I was alert for the flood of discouragement that was about to besiege me.

"Well, I don't know," he began, as though the idea might not be all that crazy. After a thoughtful silence he added,

"If he could somehow get through to the medical degree, there's a new field of specialty called physiatry having to do with rehabilitating the disabled, after surgery and strokes and so forth. That might be an area he could look into. And then there's psychiatry."

Uncle Chill's top-of-the-head response seems today of incredible prescience. Years later, after earning my medical degree, I began my residency training for the joint specialty of physiatry and psychiatry, fascinated by the interlock between the physical and emotional aspects of handicap. Ultimately I selected psychiatry as the place I could contribute most and felt most comfortable.

Since Uncle Chill refused to discourage me, Mom turned for help to our other most trusted medical person, Dr. Campbell, our ophthalmologist. On a visit for treatment of her glaucoma, she asked, "Do you know that Dave wants to be a doctor? Would you please have a talk with him and make him see how hopeless it is?"

As Mom later told me, Dr. Campbell looked horrified. "Mrs. Hartman," he replied, "I *never* could do that."

In my junior year of high school, I got the idea of writing a letter to the director of admissions of a prominent Philadelphia medical school. Mom and Dad were delighted; they, too, were eager to hear from the horse's mouth whether my ambition was feasible or nonsensical. The director wrote back promptly and shocked us all by sounding enthusiastic, saying, in effect, that he'd love to meet me and talk with me about my becoming a doctor. I could scarcely contain my elation. It was not a crazy idea after all.

I still thrill when I remember the feeling of importance that seized me as we walked across the campus of a celebrated university, an institution I might one day attend and which might actually make me a doctor. I quivered with excitement. Finally, we were sitting in the admissions director's office, and now the answer would come.

For an unrelieved hour, scarcely asking me a single question, the director kindly but sternly listed the reasons no blind person could hope to become a doctor. He has to peer into microscopes, pick up subtle differences in color of the tongue and throat, and on and on through many duties I didn't understand. He told me of a woman with disabled limbs who had convinced his school to give her a chance at medical training. "We admitted her," the director told me. "We took the *risk* of admitting her. Then two years later she realized she couldn't do it, and quit." He paused significantly. "That risk kept someone else from becoming a doctor. Medical school is very expensive and the need for doctors is very great. It's terribly important that we admit people we know can make it."

No way could I, a zealous, single-minded, self-centered teen-ager, be swayed by such abstract societal considerations. At the end I pleaded, "But can't you take a chance on me?"

In the regretful tone of a concerned uncle, yet with maddening firmness, he said, "No. We can't risk wasting a position in a medical school."

In the death march across that campus back to our car, I struggled to see something in the darkness, the black picture of the rest of my life. I could not ever be a doctor. The admissions director, the court of no appeal, said it couldn't be done. I could never become the true me. I'd always have to be someone else, a stranger. My chest felt crushed. My heart hurt. So this, I remember saying to myself, is why they use the word "brokenhearted."

I cried that whole night.

I must interject here that toward the end of my second year of medical school, I had to direct a written inquiry to that same admissions director, who was in charge that year of administering the "national boards" in our region, a standardized exam that all medical students across the country must take. At the end of his reply he penned a

David Hartman, at two years old, in a photo taken by his father.

The Hartman family inspects what Santa brought. Dave is three and had been wearing glasses for more than a year.

Eight-year-old Dave, with his mother, boards a plane for Boston and the eye surgery that failed to save his sight. (*Photo by Fred W. Hartman*)

After the operation Dave appears to enjoy playing to the camera. (*Photo by Fred W. Hartman*)

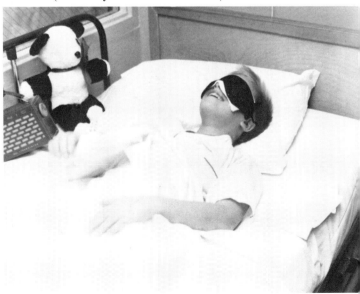

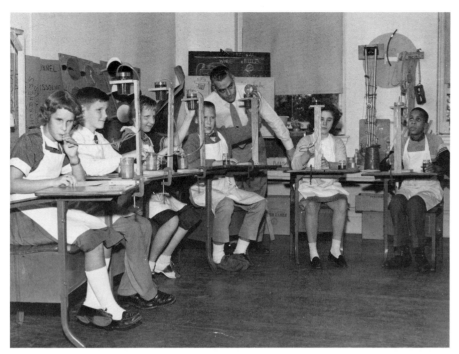

In science class at Overbrook School for the Blind, Dave's teacher inspects the twelve-year-old's experiment. (*Photo by Fred W. Hartman*)

The sparse dormitory at Overbrook. (*Photo by Fred W. Hartman*)

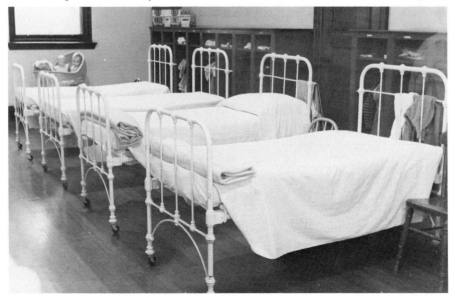

Dave, eleven years old, winning a wrestling match at Overbrook—and enjoying it. (*Photo by Fred W. Hartman*)

Racing at a swim meet in 1963. (*Photo by Fred W. Hartman*)

What's wrong with this photo? Dave, thirteen, and his sister Bobbie, sixteen, switched positions on their bicycle built for two so that Dave is steering. (*Photo by Fred W. Hartman*)

Dave, at sixteen, displays the merit badges that qualified him as an Eagle Scout in 1965. (*Photo by Fred W. Hartman*)

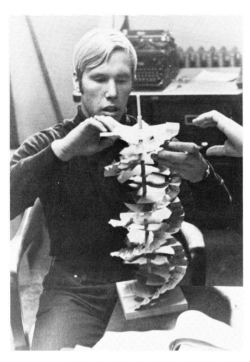

In biology class at Gettysburg College, Dave studies a model of a DNA molecule. (*Photo courtesy of Public Relations Dept., Gettysburg College*)

The president of Gettysburg College congratulates Dave upon his graduation. (*Photo courtesy of Public Relations Dept., Gettysburg College*)

Cheri's and Dave's wedding day, 1973.

Preparing for the film, *Journey from Darkness*, a two-hour TV dramatization of Dave's struggle to enter medical school, Dave instructs actor Marc Singer on how to use a cane. (*Photo by* TV GUIDE)

As Cheri and humorist Art Buchwald listen, Dr. Hartman accepts the Anne Thompson MacDonald Award given by Recordings for the Blind for outstanding achievement. (*Photo courtesy of Dept. of Public Relations, Temple University Health Sciences Center*)

notation that he remembered our conversation several years earlier, and that he was happy to see I hadn't taken his advice. I liked and admired him for that. It confirmed what I felt even on that unhappy day I visited him: that his office speech was no doubt painful to him as well as to me, contained not the faintest hint of ill will, and was a sincere attempt to help me avoid frustration and unhappiness. Just as my mother's skepticism had always been.

✕✕ 9 ✕✕

Wayne

One summer afternoon my best school-and-college-days friend, Wayne Hey, whom I valued for his bluntness among many other qualities, sat down in a beach chair next to me at our swimming club and said in a tone of mock sympathy, "Dave, I don't often feel sorry for you, but I do today. In the pool I just saw some of the prettiest girls in bikinis that I've ever seen."

I ingested that without comment, then headed for the pool, returned dripping a few minutes later to my beach chair, and said to Wayne, emulating his mock sympathy: "Wayne, I don't often feel sorry for you, but I do today. In that pool I just bumped into some of the prettiest girls in bikinis I've ever felt."

What that recollection illustrates is my belief, mentioned earlier, that everybody—everyone in the world, no matter how perfectly endowed—is handicapped. At that pool, I was handicapped, but so was Wayne. The incident also illustrates, however, that a handicap can be a strength as well as a shortcoming.

That idea began exploding in my mind during the summer preceding my final year in high school. In the spring

Wayne and I had gone on a church retreat and at the end of the stay an engaging young minister, Reverend Calvin Carey, had a talk with me. "Dave," he said, "I run a day camp in the summer for mentally retarded kids. I'd like to find you a job at the camp. The kids might especially identify with you."

The minister made it clear my job would be unpaid, but that was okay. At least he was asking me to do something, to show I could do a job. The previous summer I'd broken my fanny trying to find work, and nobody would give me any.

For the first day of camp, I'd planned to take the bus that was to pick up campers, but Wayne said, "I'll drive you out there." Wayne stayed for the day, helping out, and at the end of it the minister—whom by this time we were calling Cal—said. "Wayne, what are you doing this summer?"

"Looking for a job."

"We need someone to take care of the animals. I'll pay you five hundred dollars."

I was glad for Wayne, but I have to admit I felt slighted —in fact, deprived and hurt. I'd reorganized my whole life, cleared out my whole summer, for the privilege of doing volunteer work at the camp. Wayne just offered to drive me there, and fell into a paying job. I could feed the animals as well as he, but the blind guy doesn't get asked. My resentment wasn't against Wayne, certainly, and not even against Cal, for whom I had developed a strong affection. Cal's real reason, perfectly understandable although perhaps unconscious, was that he had no experience in judging what a blind person could and could not do.

In a sense, I had to invent my own job. Because I was a varsity wrestler at school, Cal assigned me to teach wrestling. But wrestling, a sport of quick reaction and surprises, was not best suited for the children of this camp, who often lacked muscular coordination as well as quickness of mind.

The person who helped me most—indirectly—in creating an interesting job was the young woman who served as camp sports director. Being of an executive turn of mind, she pursued her supervisory responsibilities by sitting on her ass all day, doing absolutely nothing, so I began doing some of her problem solving, some of her counseling of counselors, and seeing to it that groups of kids moved from one sports activity to another on time. Counselors and the specialists in charge of this sport or that would have questions about how to adapt a sport or game to the limitations of retarded kids, and they began bringing their questions to me. I'd had no more experience in it than they, but I played it by ear and we all learned a lot.

Next summer Cal asked me to come back, this time with pay of $500. Even though I'd shown—or thought I had— that I could fill the job of sports director, he brought in another young woman to serve as codirector, this time explaining that a man-woman pair might be effective. Fine. But she, too, had a penchant for hanging back, letting me do everything, and Cal soon saw that he was paying for two people when clearly one could do the job.

What bothered me was that a sighted person could get a job first, then go on to prove his or her competence or lack of it—the risk was the employer's. The blind person, on the other hand, always has to prove himself first—and, more often than not, doesn't even get a chance to. Sometimes I feel like I've spent most of the best months and years of my life proving, proving, proving—and even now when I've accomplished what I was previously told was impossible, I have to keep on proving, proving, proving. On some days it's discouraging.

My typical day that summer would start off with all the kids and counselors in a circle and I'd lead exercises, like jumping jacks. Then the camp would split into small groups for games, like dodge ball—players in a circle throwing the ball, trying to hit the dodger in the middle. It was a good game for these kids because it was simple, had excitement, and offered a simple means of achieving success. In fact the game was so alluring that sometimes I'd have to remind counselors that the dodger should be one of the children, not the counselor. Voices told me most of what was going on, but I also depended on volunteered feedback, and had to train counselors to give it to me. In calisthenics, one might say, "Dave, you're going too fast," or "too slow."

Wayne would often serve as a pair of eyes. He was good at it. Learning to depend on him for certain observations while reserving independence in decision making was valuable training for me. In medicine, doctors depend constantly on other people's observations—X rays, electrocardiograms, lab tests, all sorts of nurses' reports—and I have to rely on the reports of others a little more than most, yet make my own decisions.

Wayne was helpful in other ways—ways that have changed and helped set the direction of my life. The main way he helped was in permitting me no illusions, no unjustified allowances. Sometimes an ingratiating counselor or visiting parent would take my hand and say, "Dave, you're doing a tremendous job." Sometimes I'd overhear a modification that I hated: "Wow, for a blind person, he's doing a terrific job." Wayne might hear it, too. Later, apologizing for "being a bastard" (he'd feel really guilty about being blunt and truthful with me), he'd say, "They're being nice to you, but, I may as well tell you, that sports area doesn't look so hot. Nothing's going on. Some kids are just loafing. I think you could be doing much more."

Nobody was as straightforward with me as Wayne. He allowed that the job I was doing was adequate, because it was, but "tremendous" or "terrific" it was not, except in terms of that unacceptable cop-out, "for a blind person." I've always craved an accurate judgment of how I'm doing; I didn't want to evade my blindness, pretend it was not there.

One night, driving home from camp with Wayne, a colossal thought struck me. Blindness was a disadvantage— *at camp*. But in other kinds of activities it might actually be an advantage. I had been thinking about my growing but still unclear ambition to become a doctor, and I suppose I was made all the more uneasy about it by Wayne's frank estimate of how I was doing at camp. I was feeling down. If I couldn't run a game of dodge ball among mentally retarded kids without the help of someone else's eyes, how in the world could I run a medical practice, order highly trained people around in an operating room? Suddenly, perhaps in a flash of memory of Uncle Chill's suggestion when I was still in eighth grade, came the idea that blindness, a handicap in many fields of medicine as it was in day camp, could be an advantage in psychiatry. I felt I could bring a special empathy to patients coping with such stresses as phobias and difficulties in interpersonal relationships as well as to emotional problems of the disabled. My handicap would be a strength. Instead of competing with sighted people on their ground, I could create a ground of my own where *they* would have to work twice as hard to keep up with *my* understanding.

The road to validating that idea has been winding and rocky and long. Along the way I have developed a companion to my precept that everybody is handicapped. The companion idea is that the people most likely to succeed are those who have a knack for turning their handicaps into advantages.

More than anyone else, Wayne pointed me in the direction of believing that.

My earliest recollection of knowing Wayne Hey was as a second- or third-grader. I hated him. Immediately. We had a fight over who was entitled to the next turn on the school-yard swing, and he bent my glasses. My next awareness of

him was years later, in sixth grade, long after I'd lost my
sight and left our neighborhood school to go to Overbrook.
At Sunday school one day he offered to walk me home. I
told him my sister waited for me. The following week I
heard my name called up a flight of crowded stairs in a
strange, squeaky voice. It turned out to be Wayne's. He
was mimicking my sister, still wanting to walk me home.

Wayne and I would see each other at Boy Scout meetings, too, but I wasn't overly anxious to know him because
athletics didn't interest him much and I'd heard he was just
a so-so student; practical jokes and having a good time
appeared to be his main interests. I perceived at Scouts,
however, that in whatever he took up there he went to great
lengths to excel. He was extremely competitive. As our
acquaintance began to develop and he learned I was something of a "star" wrestler, he threw himself into body building and learning the finer points of wrestling. (Today he's
a well-built guy with an athlete's arms, shoulders, and legs.
Wayne is about six feet tall, two inches or so taller than I.)

Sometimes after church Wayne would say, "Why don't
you come over and we'll play cards, or look at TV?" I'd say
okay, for lack of any other plan, but that would be it; I
wouldn't make moves to advance the friendship. His
mimicking Bobbie, which I first took as teasing, bespoke
an eagerness to attract my attention and friendship, and
something about that eagerness put me off. Also I sensed a
threat. Don Jarvis, who had just moved to a house right
behind mine and was becoming my best friend, had previously been Wayne's neighbor—and best friend. I feared
Wayne as potentially serious competition for Don's friendship. Blind kids have trouble making new friends, and I
wanted and needed Don as one.

At Scouts, Wayne and I became partners in our training
as junior lifesavers. That can be a real enemy maker, rough
stuff. Wayne was rough on me—and expected me to be
rough with him—but there was a respect and caring to his

roughness. He was determined to become the best life-saver he could, and expected me to do the same. He made no allowances for my blindness. His toughness was a kind of kindness that I had not experienced with anyone except my father.

One day I began to wonder why I had resisted friendship with Wayne. I began to say to myself, "He's really a nice guy. He likes me, not because I'm a blind weirdo or something, but because he likes *me*."

I have often observed that people who make the most of treating me as an unfortunate often turn out to be more handicapped than I am, suffering from some emotional emptiness that they try to fill by taking possession of me.

Wayne was just the opposite of people who try to make themselves feel good by doing things for me. Wayne didn't do things for me. He'd push me, challenge me into doing my own things. He'd take the trouble to figure out ways for me to do things, just as Dad always did.

For example, during our high-school summers, Wayne would pick up money by mowing lawns. I couldn't mow lawns, had no way to make money, and Wayne sensed my frustration. One day he had a fairly big yard job and took me along. He tied the end of a clothesline around a tree and the other end to the mower, and told me to start mowing. As I mowed around a large circle, the rope kept wrapping around the tree, leading me and the mower on a spiral path closer and closer to the tree until a large section of the lawn was mowed. Meanwhile, Wayne was doing other chores. While his brilliant invention had some imperfections, I did get some of the lawn done and we did enjoy working together and Wayne did give me part of his fee, roughly proportional to the work I got done.

Wayne expected a great deal of himself—and then had the bloody nerve to expect the same thing of me. We'd get into fights over it. One day at camp when nothing much was doing, he said, "Let's go hike up that hill." The hill was scarily steep. If you began sliding down it, I don't know what would stop your fall except smashing into a tree, which I wouldn't see to grab. I don't like physical risks. That hill probably wasn't as dangerous as it felt to me, but I'm constantly nervous—about falling into holes, off unexpectedly deep curbs, of being hit by a car.

"Wayne," I complained in a trembling voice I tried to make brave, "why do we have to go up this way? There's another way to get to the top, the way we take the campers."

"That way is too long. This is direct. Don't be a chicken."

I was furious at him for putting me through this. Suppose he fell and broke his leg. I couldn't run and get help. But that fool knew damn well he wouldn't break his leg and he was sure I wouldn't break mine. He seemed oblivious to possible consequences. He believed in me, which during those agonizing minutes I deeply resented him for. He projected his self-confidence on me, not giving me an inch of special allowance, and I hated him for it. And when we finally got safely to the pinnacle of the hill, I loved him for it.

At times his zest and abilities made me feel inadequate, and then he'd say something surprising that would turn my feeling upside down. During our friendship he changed from a nonathlete to an enthusiastic and often good athlete. He became a wrestler, a swimmer. I taught him to play chords on the guitar and he soon surpassed me on it. We'd play chess and cards (with a Brailled deck). I usually stayed ahead of him in chess, but not because he didn't try to pulverize me. At a blue moment one day, I commented that I wished I could learn new activities as fast as he, wished I could excel at so many things the way he did. To my astonishment he replied, "In all the things you do, Dave, I've had to compete with you. The reason I've developed in all that stuff is because you challenged me."

The one competition in which Wayne had it all over me—and to Wayne, everything is competition—was the struggle for girls. Girls just flocked to him, or so I felt. My reaction was bald envy, jealousy. We'd often go out on double dates, but when I sensed my date falling in love with Wayne, I'd want to explode in a white fury. Why couldn't he just cool his personality a little bit? It was bad enough he had the advantage of sight, without having to sugar it with charm.

One unforgettable time on a double date Wayne decided to invoke his abominable lack of physical fear. We were strolling through an amusement park when Wayne said, "Hey, that ride looks like fun. Scary!"

I moaned. "Listen, Wayne, rides don't turn me on. They just don't do anything for me except make me nauseated. Like I really get sick."

"Dave, you're a chicken. You've got to push yourself."

I hated to in the presence of our dates, but I explained to Wayne that I thought my nausea was because I couldn't see which way was up.

Wayne challenged, "I'll tell you what. We're going up on that ride and I'm going to keep my eyes shut."

The ride was a horror, made infinitely worse by the generosity of the attendant at the controls. He wanted to be nice to the blind kid, I guess, so he kept the ride going for fully twenty minutes.

Again, Wayne outdid me. Coming off the ride, I didn't quite puke, but Wayne sure did. When he could finally bring himself to speak, he sputtered, "Yeah, you're right."

Wayne was interested in what I *could* do and excel in, not the many things I couldn't do. What bound us together was not a common interest in particular activities but a common need to be best in what each of us chose to do. Maybe a neurotic need, but a binding one nevertheless.

Wayne influenced the shape and direction of my life as much as my family did. He was as close as a brother, a kind of twin brother. Eventually I met Cheri, whom I was soon to marry, and Wayne met Peggy, whom he was soon to marry. As a foursome we hit it off quite well, but not the way Wayne and I did with one another, and our new lives had to get in the way of the old. Cheri, while feeling a deep affection for Wayne, admitted to me that she couldn't feel entirely comfortable with him. For years Wayne and I told each other everything—*everything*—and Cheri didn't feel quite right fully exposed to a third person. Peggy must have felt somewhat the same. When life took Wayne to Michigan for his surgical training, we drifted away from each other. I miss what our friendship was, but both of us had to move on.

10

Anybody Around?

In September 1968, I became a student at Gettysburg College, where both of my parents had been schooled; in fact, where they met. It's a quiet school on a relaxed, spread-out campus of ivy-coated brick buildings that border along the main downtown street of a quiet, proud, historic town, Gettysburg, Pennsylvania. Among its minor but significant advantages for me was that the campus layout is orderly, a simple geometric design of walkways linking the buildings. The place gave me confidence in getting about with minimal help.

The freshman dorm was home during my first year. In the spring I joined the Sigma Chi fraternity and took meals there. My second year, I found a small apartment above a popular restaurant called the Lamp Post on the main street directly across from the campus. It had the advantages of privacy, easy access to low-cost meals, and proximity to campus buildings. The only trouble was that I had to cross that busy main drag at least twice a day, usually during the hours of heaviest traffic.

Just thinking of that, in fact, brings back a vivid, terrifying memory. One early evening the sidewalks were deserted because rain was pouring mercilessly. I dreaded stepping off the curb. The rain slashed down and thunder rolled, cracked fearsomely, drowning out the sound of approaching cars. "Anybody around?" I called, sensing nobody would answer, and nobody did. "Anybody around?" I called again and again. Nobody around. Should I just run for it? I knew the rule about wearing light-colored clothes when walking on highways in darkness. I was wearing my Sigma Chi parka, the fraternity color—dark blue. I *had* to get across. I was hungry, cold, drenched, lonely, and desperately needed my evening to cram for an exam. "Anybody around?" Wielding my white cane in the air like a swordsman gone mad, I plunged into the street, just kept going, expecting any moment to be smashed dead, yet somehow believing that it was not supposed to end like this.

Moments later I sat in my room dripping, exhausted, in disbelief that I was there. Unharmed. Alive. Sitting there was one of those rare moments when I do ask myself bitterly, "Damn, damn, why does it have to be me? Why do I have to put up with this crap all the time when other people don't?"

Yes, I suppose a Seeing Eye dog would help prevent some of those occasional agonies. To the best of my knowledge, Seeing Eye dogs are not specifically trained to avoid automobiles, but I'm sure they hold their owners back when cars are coming, because all living things make a sincere effort to save their own asses. But at Gettysburg a dog seemed simply too much of a bother for that neatly laid-out campus. And later, in medical school, when I had to contend with big-city streets, the fear crossed my mind that a dog would be unwelcome in a hospital, and I had enough obstacles to acceptance without adding an animal to them. So to this day I have never had a Seeing Eye dog. Maybe someday I'll change my mind.

Tucked away in my closet I have a box of papers that are the product of those college years. There's an eight-page essay (for English class) on Thoreau and transcendentalism. I did a thick paper on sedums, perennial herbs that thrive in the desert, and another on the meaning of differences in eye color of drosophilas—fruit flies. And there's an analysis of an experiment comparing the rates of utilization of fatty acids against those of carbohydrates in red and white muscle tissues. Still another, a long one, titled "Carl Rogers and Client-Centered Therapy" for Psychology 341, Professor Platt.

People ask me how I studied and did papers, and my answer is "When?" All through high school and college I kept revising my methods, flying by the seat of my pants. Generally, in doing a college paper I'd Braille it first. I have a Braille writer, an embossing machine with a keyboard, shaped something like a typewriter. I can Braille with the speed of a slow typist, slightly faster than writing by hand. The problem with Braille is that after you've done a page, you can't change it. You can't squeeze extra words or corrections between the lines. I'd punch a hole in the margin to indicate a correction, then I'd do my correction on another sheet in advance of re-Brailling the whole paper. I'd type the finished version.

At Overbrook, where typing is normally taught in seventh grade, I asked to take it in third, and the teacher consented. I can type quite rapidly, but not too accurately, and my spelling is awful. After typing a paper, I'd get a reader to proofread it and correct mistakes, including grammatical errors. At first I worried that this was cheating, then I decided that if a paper was not for English class I wasn't cheating, just making it more presentable. I found that I was quite proficient at organizing information for a complex paper; the trouble came with pushing that information through smooth, expressive sentences. I also found that just about everybody else had that same trouble.

Textbooks not available in Braille editions—and in college, most were not—would be taped for me by Recordings for the Blind. Sometimes they already had a master tape of a book I wanted, so they'd just run off a copy for me and send it in a few days. A book that had to be taped especially for me, however, might take several weeks. And in medical school, one basic medical textbook that students simply call by its author's name, Harrison, took almost two years to complete. The printed version is 2000 pages long, packed tightly with technical terms. I have it on sixty tapes, four hours a tape. That represents 240 hours of reading by patient, generous, erudite volunteers. On occasion, when I needed a book in a hurry and Recordings for the Blind had no master tape to copy it from, a local Philadelphia organization, Volunteer Service for the Blind, would rush a taping of it. Volunteer Service also Brailled books for me and others, as did the American Printing House for the Blind in Louisville, Kentucky.

In using textbooks on tape, there's no way of scanning quickly for review, as speed-readers can. You've just got to sit there and listen. But there is a system of "indexing" that enables the blind researcher to pluck the section on kidney disease out of 240 hours of tape. Each tape is marked (in Braille) with the page numbers it represents from the original book. Within the tape, the beginning of each printed page is "marked" by a tone, which at high speed becomes a beep. So if a printed index says that kidney disease begins on page 79, and page 79 is on a tape that begins with page 61, I speed that tape through my machine until I hear the eighteenth beep—and that's page 79. Neat? Yes. But ever so slow and laborious, especially if all you want is a single fact or simply the name of a disease or drug.

After many trials I settled down to an elaborate method

of taking notes during class lectures. It involved three tape recorders. In class, while the prof was talking and scribbling on his blackboard, I'd whisper notes into a miniature tape recorder in my hand. Sometimes I'd tape the whole lecture. That night at home, I'd replay the lecture or my impromptu notes and dictate more selectively into another miniature recorder, producing an outline that might appear in any student's notebook. Finishing that, I'd retape the outline on a large reel of tape, adding it to previous lecture outlines. That would be my permanent "notebook," each tape indexed with Braille tabs, and each lecture identified with beeps. In medical school, where pressure is far greater than in college, a day's lectures, perhaps six hours, might require twelve or more additional hours to "file" in my notebook. That was every day. If I let up on the grueling pace a single day, I would probably fall hopelessly behind in my work.

These peculiar study methods were a leading reason for my moving out of the dormitories and into that small apartment above the Lamp Post. In the freshman dorm I had the worst kind of roommate for me—a fellow who'd always say everything was fine when clearly it wasn't. He'd refuse to come up with honest feedback, which everyone needs, but I more than most people. He was a big rough, tough guy on a football scholarship, immersed in the role of big man on campus, deeply wanting to be cool but failing at it.

My study method of sometimes talking notes into a recorder while reading a textbook bugged the hell out of him. I'd always ask whether he was studying or thinking and whether he'd be bothered by my note taking. "Oh, no, not at all," he'd insist. I'd continue as quietly as I could. Then later a dorm neighbor would tell me that my roommate was immensely pissed off, that he walked past me in the hall and gave me the finger, supposedly to amuse everyone else. Eventually he moved out, leaving the room all to me, which suited me perfectly.

In an early semester I signed up for a biology lab. Knowing I was blind, the surprised biology professor, A. Ralph Cavaliere, called me to his office to say that, really, a lecture course in biology would be instructive enough.

"But I plan to major in biology," I told him.

After a tense silence—I wasn't sure if he was annoyed or stunned or what—he suggested, "Wouldn't you be better off in history? Or sociology?"

"But I want to go to medical school," I said.

"Well, I don't know," mused Dr. Cavaliere. He got up, paced his office, then left. Soon he returned, announcing, "We'll give it a try."

I liked him. He wasn't the first to think I was crazy, but he was among the first to allow me the brighter side of his doubt. Skeptical and troubled he certainly was, but he gave me a chance to prove I might be right before concluding that I had to be wrong. Before my four years at Gettysburg ended, Dr. Cavaliere, in his mid-thirties, became one of my closest faculty friends, an inspiration, and supporter.

Another young professor, Al Schroeder, after some hesitation, accepted me into his physiology class, and later into histology. Dr. Schroeder's first objection was that I couldn't see pictures and diagrams. I showed him my Braille-like drawing kit, which intrigued him. In addition to preparing drawings for me, he devoted two hours a week to working with me privately. Thanks to his commitment I got an "A" in his course, and he, too, became a close friend and rooter.

Dr. Schroeder's physiology lab was at first a frustration. Students were graded on the quality of their performance, but since we worked in pairs or groups of three or four around a lab table, the grade actually evaluated group performance. That meant that my handicap could put my partner or group at a disadvantage. I really wanted to be involved, yet, if I got too involved, I might mess up an experiment. One fellow on my team was especially helpful, always explaining, "We're doing this and this and this." But sitting for four hours just hearing about what someone else is doing is not lab.

I finally went to Dr. Schroeder and said we had to figure out a way for me to do things without slowing or jeopardizing the work of others. Schroeder thought a moment, then said he'd have just the thing for our next session.

Sure enough, he had arranged some special lab work that made me feel involved—more so than I bargained for. Schroeder had been conducting a study of the functions of the various parts of the digestive tract of the cockroach. He showed my partner how, with a fine blade, to carve around the head of the cockroach, then I was to take the insect and yank its head off. If I did it just right, the intestinal tract would come right up with it, in perfect condition.

Before being beheaded, the roaches were anesthetized with a drop of ether, which wears off quickly. I had to do my job quickly as well as accurately, otherwise the subjects would wake up and start to wiggle. After disemboweling the cockroach, I'd pass the treasured parts to my partner, who then separated the four main sections of the digestive tract, putting each into a test tube. Through color changes, we could then determine the chemical contents of each section. The experiment was easy enough for a beginning student to do and understand, but intricate enough to be interesting and to develop lab competence.

Another time we worked with turtles. We did open-heart surgery on one turtle, and Schroeder actually had me put my finger on the turtle's heart, feeling its pulsation. An exciting and memorable experience. Anesthetizing a turtle is different from anesthetizing a cockroach. The turtle is sent swiftly and gently into that sweet night by smashing its head with a hammer. It squishes a lot, but not for long. While some purists might call the turtle clinically dead simply because it was made brainless, its heart continues to beat for a considerable length of time.

During the first couple of years at Gettysburg, my time was filled with study, and not just for the obvious reason that it took me longer than others to study a given amount. Study helped cover my frustrations about dating. Yes, I had my share of dates, but I'd return to my room feeling they hadn't gone well. I'd sit down and study for an hour. The guys thought I was crazy. "Dave," they'd say, "it's Saturday night and you've been out on a date. Why don't you go to sleep?" My reason, which I couldn't tell them, was that study restored my self-confidence. I'd always known that if I put my heart into study I could get any grade I wanted. Study put me back in charge of myself and my life.

My social insecurities in college were not just with girls, of course. The reason I joined Sigma Chi was to advance the cause of feeling accepted. Once joining the fraternity, however, I encountered the old story of not only feeling uncomfortable until I felt accepted, but realizing that others were uncomfortable with me until they knew how to deal with me. I resorted to making jokes about my blindness. Jokes were very effective in relaxing people. They also gained attention, which I apparently crave, even though after gaining it I'd fret over whether I got it for the wrong reasons.

I'd walk into a room, hear a quick-freeze in conversation (which might happen upon anyone's arrival), and I'd crack, "Why doesn't somebody turn the lights on? I can't see a damn thing." Someone would ask as a bunch of us were piling into a car, "Who's going to drive?" I'd be first to answer, "I will." Everybody would laugh, encouraging me to repeat the wisecrack next time. At some point the laughter becomes automatic, habitual, indulgent, but

it's hard to put your finger on just when. Before long, someone would head me off, "Hey, Dave, you gonna drive?"
And I'd be annoyed at the feeble joke. What right has he
to claim my turf?

Inevitably, I realized that my little jokes, while at first
relaxing people, eventually fixated them on me as a blind
person, not as Dave Hartman. So I resolved to move away
from snappy one-liners during tense social moments, but
I didn't always succeed. To this day I reflexively reach for
them.

There was another kind of college fun I engaged in that
I'd like to take credit for but feel impelled to attribute to
higher authority. One night we were having a beer bash at
the fraternity, the room merry with admiring girls and lots
of laughs. I began spinning one of my sure-fire lines: that
the quantity of beer that made other guys see double had
the effect on me of making me see single. When I was sure
I had my audience, I put on the awestruck look of someone
in a mystical trance and declared, "Here it comes, I'm starting to see right now."

Some smart aleck from another fraternity asked from
across the room, "All right, Dave, how many fingers am
I holding up?"

On impulse, relying on blind luck, I snapped, "Two."

"I can't believe it," the guy muttered. "Maybe he does
see."

Realizing I'd hit the number on the head (not all that
improbable), I smugly guzzled the last out of my beer can
and, with a devil-may-care flourish, tossed the can up toward the ceiling. Suddenly from the corner came a metallic
klunk, followed by a shocked hush throughout the room.
The can had plopped directly into a wastebasket.

If truth be known, I knew that wastebasket was in that
corner, so the occurrence was less than miraculous. But
there was another time when I was sitting with a college
friend, Don Johnson, in a strange room, sipping soda out

of a paper cup. When my cup was empty, for some stupid reason I tossed it straight up in the air. It fell right into a wastebasket. Don was flabbergasted. I wouldn't think much of that either, except for an incident that once happened in high school. The teacher was out of the room, and everybody was throwing paper wads, trying to get them into her basket, and nobody could. Sitting ten feet away, I called out cavalierly, "Just tap that waste can once for me." Somebody did, and I tossed. Right in.

Three incidents like that and you do start to believe that somebody up there is keeping an eye on you. (As for the 3000 times I've tossed stuff at baskets and missed, the obvious explanation is that somebody up there has a lot to worry about and can't be watching me *all* the time.)

11

Love Is Blind

A running theme through these chapters has been that feeling pitied is the worst feeling I know. When I look back to figure out who taught me the horrors of pity, all I can think of is girls. I hear a blend of girls' voices, well-meaning girls, saying, "Oh, Dave, I'd be *glad* to go out with you." Translation: "I'd be glad to give up a real date and go out with you."

I remember one girl who interested me in my sophomore year at Gettysburg. She was very religious. The day I had the courage to ask her for a date happened to be Holy Thursday, so I said, "Hey, why don't we go to church tonight?" She said, "Fine." When I picked her up she said, "By the way, I told Miriam, the other blind student here, that you and I were going to church and asked her to come too."

Just great. I was so pissed off I don't think I said a word all the way to church as the three of us wended our way symmetrically, the sighted one in the middle, a dependent on either side hanging on like lame wings. I had anticipated the evening as a date. To her, it was "blind night at church."

Let me digress a moment to tell about Miriam. We had

nothing in common except our blindness, although over a period of time I learned to like and admire her a great deal. She was very verbal, very expressive, a talented writer (the very areas in which I feel weak), and, incidentally, she was a skilled typist. Like many artistic souls, Miriam was not overcome with love for the practical and precise—like science.

People compared us incessantly. They'd ask, "Dave, how come you're so aggressive and Miriam isn't?" Nobody would expect two people to be similar just because they were both from Texas or both majored in astronomy. People would urge me to "help" her, encourage her to be more forward, especially to urge her to join a sorority. I tried once. She listened respectfully, then told me quite straightforwardly, in effect, that she didn't want to hear all that crap. As it turned out, a few months later I quit my fraternity, finding it a phony way to relate to people. The point I'm trying to make is that my being blind and her being blind didn't automatically mean we had some great common ground.

I should add that, in my sophomore year, the school acquired a new blind freshman, a guy named Max. His family made a big point of coming to see me to ask, "What's it like for a blind person in college? What should he know?"

I said, "One of the most important things is that Max have a good social life. Good grades are great, but you can't live like a monk. You have to have a good time, too. He should join a fraternity, ask girls out."

Max learned well from my hard knocks. He joined a fraternity and had such a good time that in his freshman year he flunked out.

The lure of becoming dependent on a woman—the way we all once were on Mom—appeals to some part of every man. This is especially true of a blind man, because he's had his dependence cultivated beyond the normal share. Fortunately, I worked my way through—and learned to resist —that need, thanks to two girls, either of whom I might have wound up marrying.

Laura was probably the first girl I ever fell in love with. I adored her. She was about four-foot-eleven, tender, slightly unsure of herself, had a musical and delicate voice, and she, too, was extremely religious. Her father was an ordained evangelist minister, a rough-edged, blue-collar type who worked weekdays as a truck driver. In fact, I met Laura (who was still a high-school senior) at a religious camp.

Laura would read to me with endless patience. She'd anticipate my wants. She'd bubble over my ideas of things to do, never letting her ideas—if she had any—interfere. I could just see her happily driving me to an office every morning, picking me up every afternoon, never complaining about the empty hours in between, sitting at home sewing if I wanted to sit home, cheerily going out if I wanted to go out. Who wouldn't love her?

Two impediments blocked the growth of our relationship. First, getting to see Laura was a hassle because she lived about an hour's drive from Gettysburg, and I'd have to ask Dad or Wayne to drive to Gettysburg, then drive me to her town, then kill an evening, then drive me back. Under such handicap, courtship does not easily thrive. Second, she broke the news to me one day at the shore: "I've got to tell you, Dave, that Dad doesn't like my dating a blind person."

I was amused to find myself not angry but amused. This man, concerned for his daughter's economic future, was protecting her from starvation at the hands of a guy on his way to becoming a doctor! I learned that every time she went out with me she had to say she was going somewhere else. My own close, trusting relationship with my parents made it unthinkable to come between Laura and her father.

I just couldn't do it. Her hope lay, Laura said, in my making a trip to their house for dinner, meeting him, and making him like me.

I took a train there and spent the day. Finally I got up the nerve to ask if he'd ever met a blind person before. He replied, "Sure I have. I met a guy in downtown Philadelphia who was standing on a corner with a cane and I think a cup." Begging was all he could imagine that blind people do.

In certain ways being blind is similar to being black. You're stereotyped. But along with the similarities, there are sharp differences. Black people are demeaned, ignored, sometimes kicked aside. Race differences bring out the worst in people. In contrast, blind people bring out the politeness, kindness, solicitousness of others. Only the worst of meanies would ever be nasty to a blind person. So, in a sense, blacks are worse off than the blind. But differences or no, blacks and blind people feel a natural kinship. They are both outcasts. At the hospital I have sensed black patients accepting me as kindred, in a way, and I find that comfortable.

The first evening at Laura's home, meeting her father for the first time, I gained an insight into her. Her mother had died years earlier and her father was secure in his family role as strong man: "Get me this, get me that. The salt shaker's empty, fill it." And Laura was secure in her obedient role.

I didn't fully realize how much I viewed her in that role until weeks later when we were alone one night, talking. She was upset about something, starting to cry. I said, "Honey, come over here," snapping my fingers. Suddenly I realized I had become the master in our relationship; she now was obeying me as she always had obeyed her father. Was that good for her? Was that good for me?

The differences between Laura's world and mine became increasingly clear. Inevitably the relationship faded.

My closest brush with a marriage that didn't take place was brought on by Dolores. Dolores's family, in not-to-worry economic shape, lived on a forty-four-acre estate in Chestnut Hill, one of the world's "right" places to live. While I was an undergraduate, she, a couple of years older than I, was getting her master's degree. Girls slightly older than I attract me, maybe because my sister is two years older. When you have a slightly older sister who spends your whole childhood saying, "You'll find out for yourself when you're older," slightly older is the big time.

Everything about Dolores was wonderful and it would have been a perfect marriage. She was the most organized person I'd ever met. I remember a time when my caps were irritating the surface of my eyes and I showed her how I mixed a solution to relieve the soreness. I put the bottle at a corner of the sink, making a mental note of just where it was in relation to the faucet. I always stored things that way, with memory notes. Dolores fetched a little piece of paper, marked it, and taped it to the bottle so no one could mistake what it was. Little things like that impressed me, made me feel deeply secure. She also helped me do library research. She'd do anything I wanted, she relished taking care of me. A perfect marriage.

The only trouble was I couldn't fall in love with her. No reason I can explain. There was a certain aggressiveness, a tough exterior to her, that would make Dolores a knock-out for someone else. I liked her, in a way loved her, but couldn't get turned on. How do you explain?

I met Cheri Walker, the girl I was to marry, in my statistics class. She was a sophomore, I a junior. I knew her to be extremely bright, energetic, outgoing, and with a reputation for being slightly unpredictable and absentminded.

Also, I knew her to be petite, merry-voiced, and popular, all turn-ons for me. But maybe too popular. It never really occurred to me to give her any attention because she never offered me any, and I didn't think she was within my reach. Also, she was active in the student senate, heightening my feeling that she was entangled with affiliations and scarcely had room for another. I was Sigma Chi's representative in the student senate, where occasionally I got up to say something. But having been an officer of my high-school student council, I had concluded that student government was for the birds and I didn't take senate meetings seriously.

Then one day, out of the blue, I felt a soft hand on my arm after a senate meeting and Cheri's voice said, "Dave, I want to talk to you. I'm running for secretary of the senate and our ticket needs a candidate for vice-president. Would you run?"

I tingled with delight, even though I wouldn't consider running. Just to keep the conversation going, and to ingratiate myself with Cheri by showing an interest in her problem, I said, "Gee, a good friend of mine, Bob Klein, is in the senate and I'll be glad to ask if he wants to run." (Later Cheri told me she was hurt: "I couldn't believe you said that. I was pulling out my big move, the one excuse I had for getting to know you, and all you could say was, 'I'll talk to my friend.' I thought, Wow, I really struck out with this guy.")

The upshot of that conversation was a double date, the most confused and complicated in my life, perhaps in all of human history. I had promised Wayne that as a token of my esteem I would invite him to Gettysburg and set him up for a date with the most desirable girl on campus. At that moment, I felt the most desirable girl was Cheri, but it didn't seem quite right to set her up with him because she clearly seemed interested in me. So I decided I'd take Cheri and I'd fix Wayne up with an extremely attractive, vivacious girl who was in the class a year ahead of me. That girl said no, she was busy, so I had little choice but to offer Wayne Cheri—rather, to offer Cheri Wayne. Cheri said, "Sure, I'll go out with Wayne." Then I found a date for myself. Two days before the big day, my date said she couldn't go. So I had to go back to Cheri and ask, "Is there a girl you'd be able to set me up with?" She was able to find someone.

To further complicate this house of mirrors, the way I'd originally asked Cheri about the date was, "Would you mind a blind date with my friend Wayne?"

Cheri asked, "Do you mean a blind date, literally? Is your friend blind?"

My sense of mischief took hold of my tongue. "Yes, he is," I answered.

I told Wayne about that and we decided to go through with it. He showed up at my room early, borrowed one of my canes, and put on a pair of dark glasses so the girls wouldn't see the unmistakable liveliness in his eyes.

Wayne was marvelous. He sensed Cheri's uneasiness, at moments her awkwardness, in guiding a "blind" person for the first time, and he sensed something else. Maybe Cheri got a vibration about something not genuine in Wayne's behavior. Maybe it was that she knew nothing about Wayne except his "blindness"—whereas she knew more about me as a person—and found herself reacting to him as though blind was all he was. Wayne tried to relax her with jokes, blindness jokes. Unpracticed Cheri would lead him into a post, a chair, then apologize. He'd say, " 'Tsokay, 'tsokay, takes a while to learn it. Happens to me all the time." He said there was a telephone pole at his campus that people ran him into all the time, adding with resignation, "I use the dents on it now to measure whether I'm getting taller."

After dinner we went up to my place to play hearts with my Braille cards. Taking a leaf from my book of experi-

ence, Wayne asked Cheri to tap the wastebasket, then
tossed a beer can—*plunk*—right in.

At a moment when Wayne and I were out of the room
at the same time, we came to grips with the problem of how
to end this, how to break the shocking news to the girls
that Wayne could see. We thought of involving the guy
next door who owned a Grecian-style Sigma Chi robe. He
could come in, impressively frocked, perform a ritual, and
pronounce Wayne healed.

In the end we decided something more subtle was in
order. Wayne took off his dark glasses and put on his
regular specs, explaining to the girls that he did that every
once in a while as a fantasy, just to pretend he could see.
For a few seconds he'd make eye contact—unmistakable
pupil-to-pupil touching—with one of the girls; then, just
as he observed her tensing up, his eyes would go general
and vague again. Cheri became suspicious. Then his eye
contact became so direct that she knew beyond doubt that
he *could* see.

Cheri started laughing. For some reason I started laughing. Wayne started laughing. Cheri started laughing louder.
My date was perfectly silent until finally she asked, "What's
so funny?"

From then on, something relaxed between Cheri and me.
I became the object of most of her conversational attention
during the rest of the evening, and every once in a while
she'd touch my knee with that small, soft hand of hers,
which I found surprisingly thrilling.

The funny thing about that whole laughing experience—
actually, the part that was not funny—was that it left me
a little depressed. Wayne could say, "Now I'm blind. Ab-
racadabra, now I'm sighted." I couldn't. No matter how I
excelled in classes, or how many guys I pinned in wrestling,
I still had the antisexual stigma of blindness. My blindness
is what girls knew about me first, and, in most cases what
they continued to think about when they thought about

me. I've daydreamed suddenly announcing I could see and watching girls who had pushed me aside suddenly wishing they hadn't. Who would I tell first? Would I pretend for a little while that I still couldn't see, then spring it at a perfectly timed moment? Would I make macho advances at girls who had been turned off by my blindness, now turn them on—then enjoy the triumph of walking away from them cold?

That depression I felt was inescapable. I laughed, but couldn't laugh it away. In the days that followed I was forced to think about it. For the first time I was struck in the face with the knowledge, which this time I had to accept, that I really wanted to see. I further realized and accepted that I had spent a lot of my energy since the age of eight repressing—hiding from my own awareness—that desire and that knowledge.

A couple of days later I received a letter from Wayne with a long passage intended for Cheri. Based on his long and intimate experience in dealing with me, he wanted to critique Cheri's behavior when she thought he was sightless. (Clearly, Wayne had a premonition that Cheri and I were destined somehow for each other.) Wayne pointed out to Cheri that during the time she thought he was blind she was overly friendly, overly outgoing, patronizing, then as soon as he revealed he could see, "you began treating me like an ordinary guy."

For Wayne the evening was enlightening because, even though he had made a best friend of a blind person for years and had learned as well as anyone to relax and make normal demands of the friendship, our little prank gave him the singular opportunity to be on the receiving end of sighted behavior toward the blind.

A couple of weeks later the three of us enjoyed an uninhibited talk about the experience and Wayne's letter. In it, Cheri made some valid points that canceled out some of Wayne's. For one thing, Wayne wasn't blind, and Cheri had sensed something peculiar all evening; her inability to account for her peculiar feeling may have contributed to her overreaction. Second, Wayne was, after all, a blind date; she'd never met him, knew nothing about him, so there was little to react to except the most conspicuous fact about him, that he was "blind."

That defense rang true because Cheri had learned a good deal about me—observing me in classes, in student meetings—before we made personal contact, and, once we did, I never had the feeling that she was preoccupied with my blindness. In any case, Cheri, who found Wayne's letter partly helpful, partly upsetting, was made aware from that moment on that if she was to become closely involved in a blind person's life, she'd have to become finely tuned to the subtleties of blind/sighted interaction. So aware has she since become of those subtleties that Cheri has been giving talks to community groups on how to deal effectively with blind and otherwise handicapped people.

Cheri and I first dated by ourselves three evenings after that double date, on a memorable Friday, when I asked her to a student production of *How to Succeed in Business Without Really Trying*. The show was great, made all the better by Cheri's instinctive ease at whispering to me the few visual stage bits necessary to understand the hilarious lines. She had a sense for not telling me any more than necessary. Even more impressive than that, she had a way of leaning cozily into my shoulder, the better to do her whispering. I was tempted to put my arm around the back of her seat. Should I? Shouldn't I? Would we get cozier? Would it end the whole thing?

Suddenly I realized I had the aisle seat and she might be leaning into me to peer around some guy's head in front of us. I asked, "Would you see better if we changed seats?" She said, "I would." As we switched, I just left my arm around her chair. "Boy," she said, "that was quite a move."

I was startled. Her voice was smiling, but I felt like my

pants had fallen down. Should I leave my arm there? Or say I was sorry? Or just quietly take it away? I think I left it there, but it certainly slowed me down. She wasn't quite as absentminded as I thought she was.

In the days that followed, Bill Dundon, a friend across the hall, began calling me "High School Harry" because of the tiny plots I'd hatch in my eagerness to see Cheri. I'd try to figure out when she'd be likely to pass the candy machine, and I'd just happen to be there. I'd find any excuse to bring or return something to her dorm room. Telling this would embarrass me, except I was soon to learn that Cheri was playing High School Harriet. She'd see me way across campus, dash across the grass, stop just short of me along the walk, and say, "Oh, hi, Dave," seeming mildly pleased over our accidental encounter.

The following week I took her to see *Jesus Christ Superstar*, the night before our big breakthrough. A dorm was running a discotheque night. I didn't ask Cheri to it, in keeping with my long-standing policy, advised by my sophisticated friends, of never asking the same girl out two nights in a row. So there I was sitting up in my room not knowing whether to kick myself or to pretend that my policy was the wall, so I could kick a hole in it.

In the late evening—not even able to study, which had always been my reliable escape from social stress—I decided, damn it all, I'd just go over and knock on her door. Scared to death, but driven by impulse, I went. And knocked. Crushing silence.

I plodded back to my room, resigned to burying my head in my earphones and study-tapes. To go up, I had to walk past that party where everybody, absolutely everybody except me, was having fun. And I could have been there with Cheri. And if I had asked her, she wouldn't now be off somewhere else with somebody else. Upstairs, I lay down. Just before slipping on the earphones, a knock at my door.

There was Cheri. Her unbelievable presence was the

nearest thing to a miracle I could imagine. Even more miraculous, she told me she had been dancing at the disco with a guy named Stan—good-looking, highly popular, member of a high-status fraternity, and, needless to say, 20/20 vision, everything. Cheri told me that suddenly she realized she didn't want to be with Stan and told him she'd be back. She went outside, looked up at my window, saw that the light was out, and felt empty, crushed, just as I had been when no one answered her door. Then she thought, "He doesn't need a light!" She came upstairs and knocked.

There I was.

There she was.

By the following spring I had long ago traded in the advantages of Dolores for the allure of Cheri. Still—was Cheri the right one? I loved her, but was this the *real* love of my life? How was one to know? Whom do you ask? I asked a college counselor, who said, "Don't question it. Just decide through feeling and experience." That was nice, but not too specific. What made me decide was a casual but compelling observation by a dorm neighbor: "Dave, the only way you can be sure she's the right one is to date every girl in the whole world for comparison."

Of course.

I bought her a corsage, took her to a steak dinner at the Dutch Pantry, and asked Cheri to marry me a year from the following June, right after her graduation. She threw her arms around me and said yes.

In roundabout ways we hear of understandable questions that people ask about Cheri: What in her psychological makeup caused her to be drawn to a blind person? Is she turned on by a mate being physically dependent on her? Before Cheri was born, was her mother bitten by a social worker? Is she afraid to be looked at?

Cheri and I can come up with only one reasonable explanation. She spent much of her early life in Venezuela where her father was stationed by an American oil company. When she was thirteen or fourteen, while North American teen-agers were going into convulsions over Elvis Presley, Venezuelan teen-agers were tearing their hair over a guitarist and passionate singer named Jose Feliciano. Jose Feliciano is blind. To Cheri, the stereotype of blindness is not a cup-rattling beggar but a sex symbol. To her, blindness ignites romance, the dreaming of impossible dreams, eroticism, worldliness, sophistication.

How could I turn down a girl with taste like that?

Cheri adds another reason why my blindness was not a handicap to our romance. She is an intense person who requires of herself that her life have a sense of direction and achievement. When she was ten years old, she wrote a "book" about her belief in God (including her doubts). Her book resolved all the major questions of the universe, human origin, and most everything else. (The book didn't go anywhere because the next year, at age eleven, her attention was diverted by learning how to dance.) (Then Jose Feliciano took possession of her.) (Until she chucked him for me.) Like most serious young people, she was hurt by her seriousness not being taken seriously by others.

Cheri tells me that by the time we met, when she was almost twenty, she had just about given up looking for a guy whose commitment to goals was the defining characteristic of his personality. She says she found that characteristic in me. Which pleased me no end and still does, because I always had the fear—and still do, sometimes—that my drive to overcome and accomplish makes me a grind and a bore. Cheri and I found it easy, and wonderful, to take each other seriously when both of us had begun to think that no one ever would.

12

The Last I Remember
Was Three Rusty Nails

The day fantasy was transformed into action—the first practical move toward entering medical school—was during my junior year. Two professors, Dr. Robert Barnes, biology department chairman, and Dr. Alex Roland, chemistry chairman, dispatched seven letters to seven schools, asking if they would consider a candidate who was blind. They didn't yet write to the biggies—Yale, Harvard, Stanford. Before giving those schools a chance to shut their doors on me too soon, we wanted a sampling of response from others.

My overall college grades for four years averaged 3.8. (In the number-grade system used by Gettysburg and most colleges, the highest possible grade is 4.0, equivalent to an "A"; a grade of 3.0 equals a "B"; and on down.) In biology, I earned four years of "A"s, or 4.0. In chemistry, three semesters of "A"s were blemished by one semester of "B," for 3.75. In my nonscience courses, I applied myself a little less and earned a little less, averaging something like 3.5, midway between "A" and "B." These grades would earn a serious interview at any medical school for anyone—anyone except someone who is conspicuously different from the crowd.

In answer to the seven preapplication letters, five schools summarily slammed the door shut. The two that said they wouldn't bar me cold were Temple University (close-by in Philadelphia) and the University of California at La Jolla.

For some reason I felt that Temple was being more neighborly and polite than serious, while La Jolla must have been serious because they had no reason to be neighborly. So I decided to risk burning my bridge to Temple by asking if they'd give me an interview—really a preinterview —right away. I'd probably blow it, like ruining the first batch of pancakes, but I'd learn something about what to expect elsewhere and how to handle it. Temple agreed to see me.

I met with two doctors, John Franklin Huber and the medical school's associate dean, M. Prince Brigham. Dr. Huber was older, kind, encouraging. I demonstrated my raised-line drawing kit. It fascinated him. He asked other questions about blindness and study, blindness and doctoring, and seemed impressed with how I'd thought things through. Then, in the role division of two FBI men—the softie and the toughie: one to instill confidence, the other to shake you up—Dr. Brigham took over, with cold skepticism that told me this was going to lead to nowhere.

"Do you know how much reading a medical student has to absorb? How are you going to do it? How are you going to get between your dorm and the college buildings on hectic Broad Street? How will other students take to your talking into a tape recorder during lectures? All this special faculty help you require in college science courses, do you think you can expect that of an extremely busy medical school faculty?"

To the last question I replied, "I think I can distribute my need for special help widely enough over the faculty. If each can give me a little, I won't need a lot from anyone."

For the first time Dr. Brigham relented: "Well, I guess that's realistic."

While poking me to the wall, making me squirm, Dr. Brigham was taking a lot of trouble and seemed to care. I couldn't figure out what he thought—of me, of my prospects. If he was going to shoot me down—and I was at least half-convinced he was determined to—at least he'd taught me one thing for future interviews: I'd better anticipate every possible question and have a ready, convincing answer.

No matter how apprehensive I had already become about the barriers to medical school, somehow that real, live interview with two real, live admissions authorities made me more so. I had to know more about what I was letting myself in for, so during the January break of my junior year I signed on for a work-study project at Harrisburg State Hospital. It was a program in which students would assist psychologists and psychiatrists in collecting information from patients through interviews, and I sat in on a lot of family counseling by professional pairs—a social worker and psychiatrist.

In the course of the program I saw nothing that I didn't have total confidence I could learn to do well. That was encouraging, as was a leisure-time conversation I had with a psychiatrist, an unusually sensitive and bright Oriental. I asked what he thought about my crazy idea of going to medical school. Without hesitation he replied, "You're going to have a rough time getting into one. But if you get in, I know you can be a psychiatrist. For your residency after med school, I would happily accept you."

That was a great lift. Later I had another such opportunity, and another psychiatrist I esteemed gave me a similar lift. Something nagged at me, though, to collect still a third view, perhaps from someone in private practice and who didn't have the bias of having worked with me. Returning to Gettysburg after that exciting month, I asked to see the private psychiatrist who visited the campus a couple of times a month to counsel troubled students. I put my question to him, and the answer came readily to his lips.

"You'd never get into medical school."

"I realize that's going to be a problem," I said, "but if I do get in, do you think I could be a psychiatrist?"

"Why discuss it? You'll never get into medical school."

"I know that problem," I repeated. "But my question is, if by some miracle I got into medical school, and by some further miracle I got through it, is there anything that would bar me from performing the tasks required of a psychiatrist in private practice?"

"Yes. You'd need a medical degree, and you won't get into medical school."

But then he seemed to rerun the tape of my question through his head. "To answer your question more directly," he said, "you probably have the makings of a fine psychiatrist. No, there's virtually nothing you'd have to do that you couldn't do. But you'd never get into medical school."

Then he asked what dozens of others had asked: "Why don't you want to be a psychologist?"

"Because I love biology," I said, perhaps with an edge of exasperation. The more I studied the human body, I told him, the more it fascinated me as the most perfect machine ever made. I'd never known anything as exciting as learning its endless capacities for adapting. I wanted to deal with the mind and emotions as inseparable partners of the physical body. That's what psychiatry is about.

"Yes, that's right. But you'll never . . ."

My professors and I selected nine schools for formal applications, among them Harvard, Yale, Tulane, La Jolla, Temple, and Duke. (Drs. Barnes and Cavaliere had done their graduate work at Duke. Cavaliere was in thick with someone on the medical admissions board, and he knew that his high recommendation would at least get me respectable consideration.) A tenth was added when a friend of Dr.

Schroeder's urged, "Medical College of Pennsylvania, which used to be just for women, is now taking men, and they're especially interested in unusual types of people. They'd like Dave to apply." (Ironically, the nickname of the school had changed from "Women's" to "MCP.")

Beyond my worst expectations, the applications turned out to be a tremendous drudgery. For one thing, each school presented a different set of questions on which to base an essay. I assembled all the questions of all ten applications, figured out a single essay outline that would cover all of them, and wrote the same essay to all. It took me two days to write it; I hate writing—it makes me terribly insecure, perhaps because my parents, who were always supportive of me in almost every other way, never seemed to like anything I wrote. As I expected, my essay horrified them. I wrote it in narrative, story-telling form, explaining how my interest in science and biology and my awe of Uncle Chill evolved into an interest in medicine and eventually a determination to become a doctor. Perhaps my parents thought I should sound a little more profound and solemn, like young Sigmund Freud himself. Their reaction shook me but didn't convince me. I took my Braille manuscript back to school and read it to Cheri. She said she liked it. So I decided that's it.

Then Dad's onerous contribution began. Night after night after night he'd come home from work, finish dinner, clear the dining-room table, and spend long hours filling out those interminable, fine-print, tedious applications. With each went a check of $20 or $30 for an application fee. On his modest bank salary, $200 to $300 was an impressive chunk of money, and it later cost that amount a couple of times over to travel for interviews at schools that invited me. Not a single one of those monstrous, bewildering applications had to be returned for additional information. That's how diligent Dad was.

One Friday afternoon Bobbie drove up for my birthday

weekend from Wilmington, Delaware, where she had become a Head Start teacher. Wayne came over, too. Mom and Dad weren't yet home from work. I was bubbling over with joy at finally having reached this critical stage, evaluating what I thought to be my chances at each school. Finally I ran out of details and waited for their response.

Bobbie spoke up. What she said, according to my best recollection, was: "You know, I've been here I don't know how long and you haven't said a single word about what you'll do if you don't make it. You refuse to face the probability that no school is going to take a chance on you, and if they all turn you down, you're going to be devastated. Have you thought for one single moment what you're going to do if your dream doesn't come true?" (What she didn't say—but what I learned later she was thinking—was that in her senior year at the University of Delaware two seniors had committed suicide, that students are often inordinately affected by failures, and that she had become deeply worried by my refusal to consider the possibility of failure.)

Neither Bobbie nor I outdoes the other when it comes to hot temper, and we had one hell of a yelling and screaming match. Wayne just sat there, stunned and silent at the surprising birthday party. I stormed outside to walk around the block. I can't remember if I even stopped to grab my cane.

After a long cooling time, I returned. Mom and Dad were home now, glum and withdrawn. They knew an explosion had taken place, but respected that it was Bobbie's and mine and that they were to stay out of it. I thumped dramatically up to my room and flopped down on the bed. Soon Bobbie was at the door. Then she sat on the bed.

"I shouldn't get mad at you about this," she offered.

"But you're right," I had to say, "and that's why *I* got mad."

"I don't know who's right. But I came across so harshly, and it's your birthday, and I ruined it."

Then we hugged and kissed. We're pretty emotional that way; it's the way our family is: We always feel free to scream at one another, but, after unburdening, we always make up. I think it's very healthy.

Responses from medical schools would start coming in late fall, probably November, some in December. I couldn't wait to hear, even though no news probably signified good news—that I was not among those dropped in the first cut, before the schools narrowed down the applications to interview candidates, then further narrowed the interviewees to lively prospects and eventually to acceptances. I knew all that, but the heebie-jeebies overwhelmed me and I waited anxiously for the mail every day.

One day I walked to the post office with Cheri after waking up in a class we took together. (The course was the most boring I've ever taken. Its professor did research for an anesthesiologist and he had techniques for putting people to sleep that could have taught his boss lessons.) That walk to the post office was more nerve-racking with each passing day. Some days I'd get there, find I'd forgotten my mailbox key back at the dorm, and have to rush back to fetch it. On this day I drew out a long envelope, business-letter-size, not a note from home. The quality of the paper felt very official, and the envelope didn't have a window, so it wasn't a bill.

Cheri shrieked, "It's from Tulane!"

We ran to a corner. I ripped the flap open on the way. Under the light of a window she scanned it. Before she read me a word, I heard tears. Cheri wasn't sobbing, scarcely even crying, but I heard tears.

My first reaction was, Who the hell cares? There are nine more.

But it was worse than that. Maybe they thought it was a kindness, but it was an unexpected kick in the belly. They sent my check back. They wouldn't charge me the damn

$30, or whatever it was, for the evaluation because they wouldn't even give me one. Here I was this close to medical school—with entrance board exam scores of 705 for math and 605 for science out of a possible 800, scores that would compel an interview anywhere—and here was a major educational institution refusing to even consider me, prejudging me because I was blind. It was simply unfair. I clenched my fists and asked Cheri to read the letter. She read:

October 26, 1971

The Admissions Committee recently reviewed your application with great care. The Committee was deeply moved by your great determination and amazing accomplishments. Unfortunately, the Committee feels that in our setting your blindness would be an insurmountable handicap in fulfilling certain of the firm requirements for the M.D. degree.

It seems that a Ph.D. in clinical psychology may be a better route to follow than the M.D. degree. Have you considered that as an alternative?

I am returning your check for the application fee, since we are unable to act further on your application.

The best of luck to you in your educational plans for the future.

Yours sincerely,
The Chairman,
Committee on Admissions

Two weeks later, a similar envelope arrived from the University of California, San Diego, whose medical school is identified by the location of its campus at La Jolla. This was one of the three schools I was quite sure I would eventually be able to choose among if all the other choices dried up. What Cheri read, in a sense even more hurtful than the Tulane insult, was clearly a form rejection, the kind ground out by the hundreds:

November 12, 1971

. . . Comparing your preparation and record with those of a large number of candidates, the Admissions Committee regrets the necessity of having to inform you of your poor prospects for admission here. We believe you should be informed of this fact as soon as possible and urge you to concentrate your efforts toward achieving admission elsewhere. . . .

I was shocked. They didn't even want an interview. A chill seized me with the realization that my list of ten schools was not a list of "highly desirables" followed by "backups." Nothing was to be assumed. The whole thing could collapse. It was going to be a long, cold winter.

The next envelope came from Duke, where Dr. Cavaliere went out of his way to insure, through a friend on the admissions committee, decent consideration of my application.

Unbelievable. A form letter again:

. . . carefully considered your application . . . regrets to inform you that it is unlikely you will be accepted on the basis of competition with other applications presently in hand. . . . Since this decision was made on a competitive basis it in no way reflects on your ultimate ability as a physician.

When I told Dr. Cavaliere about "the love letter from your friends at Duke"—I was angry and didn't care how I said it—he replied dejectedly, "I couldn't promise you anything, but we tried."

For three and a half years Dr. Cavaliere had been my closest faculty friend and supporter, but gradually I realized I was seeing much less of him. Soon it became clear, or so I felt, that he was avoiding me. Later I learned he called Duke immediately after my letter arrived, pleading, "Isn't there something you can do? Can't you give this guy an interview?" The reply: "No, we're sorry." Cavaliere must have felt crushed with guilt. For four years he'd encouraged and tutored me, building my hopes up, and now may have suddenly feared he had done me a great wrong.

What amazes me, looking back at that time, is that even though my mailbox kept coughing up rejections, nothing but rejections, I kept racing to get to it every day. I'm sure a lot of people would have felt: I don't want to see another rejection, can't bear the pain of another one. If I'd had any sense, perhaps I would have felt that way; instead I just continued hoofing it over to that mailbox, heart pounding, hoping against hope that maybe today there'd be the acceptance.

Perhaps it all went back to my experience of relentlessly nagging my parents to put up the train or to get me a dog, never doubting I'd win because I knew they'd have to surrender. But this was the real world of medical admissions committees, not the child's world of trains and dogs and a loving mommy and daddy. Maybe they wouldn't surrender. They had the power to just kick me aside—and perhaps would.

Through my preinterview at Temple, I learned of a most difficult hindrance I had to contend with and remove. The decision facing an admissions committee was not simply whether I had a reasonable chance to overcome my handicap enough to make it. The number of applicants with the qualifications to make it far exceed every year the aggregate number of places in all medical schools. In the "better" schools, qualified applicants outnumber places by a staggering ratio. So the question facing an admissions committee is: Should we give a place to this high-risk candidate—no matter how impressive his previous record, no matter how appealing the social experiment—and thereby bar someone else from becoming a doctor who would be virtually sure to make it?

I insisted on my fair chance, on an equal privilege to compete based on my academic record, on not being pre-judged for my blindness by committee members who them-selves were not blind and did not know firsthand what blind people could learn to do and what they could not learn to do. But I make no claim that the decision I wanted them to make was easy.

Meanwhile, back at my dorm, where I was living again, the people closest to me were resolving their problems, lives progressing while mine stood blocked, inert. My dorm-mate, Don Johnson, very bright, had applied to a flock of dental schools and was collecting a pile of acceptances. The pickings were all his. He kept telling me, "That's only two rejections. Don't worry about it." "That's three re-jections. But don't worry, you'll get in." Then, "They're just not being fair to you, Dave. But that's only four. Someone will. You've just got to swallow hard and the next one'll be it."

Wayne Hey, who in his late college days decided that study was not so poisonous an activity after all, decided he wanted to become a surgeon. He was accepted by an osteopathic school in Philadelphia.

A close dorm friend who helped me stay in balance was Bill Dundon. I think Bill admired my single-mindedness and discipline, while I admired his frequent lack of it, which is to say his enviable talent for wringing enjoyment out of life. Joy and humor and a love of absurdity are what make Bill as precious as anyone I know.

With every rejection, Bill would reassure me, "Listen, Dave, if you don't get in, at least we'll have a good drunken brawl out of it." Or if he caught me feeling really down after one of those rejection letters, he'd let me stew a bit, mutter a few oaths of his own, then suddenly burst out in a laugh and say, "Wouldn't it be great if you got a letter saying, 'The Admissions Committee appreciates that you've busted your ass for seven years and earned better grades than anybody, but we regret to inform you . . .' They might even put the wrong name at the top, or, better still, address it 'Dear Appplicant.' "

Bill saved my spirit more than once by helping me see these rejections not just as my defeats but as someone else's stupidity, and, best of all, getting me to laugh at their absurdity.

We were deep into December, and Christmas was going to be a misery. In my head I was already packing for home when hope burst into my prospects. Two letters arrived, one from Yale, the other from Harvard. Wouldn't it be fantastic, my head surged as Cheri's fingers ripped open the flaps of those envelopes, if one—or, oh, my God, both!—of these most competitive and choosy of schools said, "Sure, we admire the hell out of what you've done and we're dying to have you."

Well, neither said quite that. Yale said, in fact, that they'd decided that they couldn't accept me for medical school, but that they'd like me to come up to New Haven to talk about "alternate plans."

Great, I thought bitterly. They've prejudged me like all the rest, except that they feel guilty about it, so they've cooked up the bright idea of my taking clinical psychology and now they want to talk me into it. Okay, I'll go! At least they're offering to talk to me. Maybe I can talk them out of their plan and into mine. The interview—the simple courtesy of inviting me to meet them face-to-face—is all I ask of any of them.

The envelope from Harvard was even better. No sorries, no warnings, no hemming and hawing at all. Just a straight application for an interview. Whether they were doing it out of some felt obligation to go through the route with me, I didn't know, but the interview was what I wanted, and they were offering it.

The cover letter from Harvard said I didn't have to go all the way to Boston for the interview; if I preferred, they'd arrange for my interview in Pennsylvania. I decided without question that I'd go to Boston. Dad agreed. Mom protested. The train trip and expenses for Dad and me would be at least a hundred dollars, plus Dad's lost time from work. That's a lot of money and time just thrown away, she pleaded, if I could have the same thing at home. (An unspoken implication, of course, was that it was all the more thrown away because nothing was going to come of all this. Why not go into clinical psych?)

"I'll use my own money," I responded. Years earlier, my grandparents had given us a gift of cash to help pay for my operations. A small amount of it remained unspent and was banked in my name.

Dad told Mom he thought that was reasonable. I knew, however, that he was the kind of guy who'd say that, then just forget it. I tried to explain to Mom that, if the chance of making it into Harvard could be increased the thinnest bit by going up there, it would be worth it. Also, I wanted to meet the people who would make the decision.

I have always found that I have more impact when I meet skeptics face-to-face, whether it's Laura's truck driver father, or a director of a camp for the retarded, or Harvard. More often than not, they're nervous about their own social ineptitude when it comes to dealing with blind people, while they claim to be addressing the issue of what blind people can and cannot learn to do. I know that, meeting people face-to-face, I can usually put that fear to rest, so we can address ourselves to the real question: whether or not I can do the job. And I also know that if I depend on someone else to argue my case for me—leaving that social fear unmentioned and hanging in the air—I'll lose every time.

That winter Bobbie was dating a Harvard alumnus who told me that his dorm roommate's father—I'll call him Dr.

Burns—was a prominent member of the medical school faculty. Bobbie's friend volunteered to write to the doctor about me. Gratefully I said, "Everything helps."

When I got up to Boston early in January, guess who the interviewer was: Dr. Burns. He spent a full hour asking me questions, leaving me puzzled, bewildered. Not a single question about my blindness, about study methods, skills I had acquired or couldn't acquire. He asked mostly about current affairs, particularly about hunger in Biafra. I didn't know a damn thing about Biafra. I couldn't afford to know. Since I can't pick up a newspaper and breeze through it, I had learned to be selective about the use of my time.

His questions about Biafra stemmed from the fact that, at Gettysburg, in addition to my studies I had been working with other students on a plan for schoolwide coordination of fund-raising efforts for good causes—including Biafra. Actually, because of it I think we raised more money for Biafra than we would have if all the good causes had remained in individual competition. But helping put that plan into effect was all I could handle. I couldn't become an expert on Biafra, too.

Dr. Burns turned to medical subjects. He asked me if I knew anything about transplants and grafts. I said, "A little." He explained that those were the fields of his specialty and sprang a word on me that I'd clearly never heard. Then, after exposing my fields of ignorance, he exposed one of his own, saying benignly, "Well, I'm sure you're not the first blind person to go through medical school, are you?"

"I don't know of any other," I replied.

"Well then," he said, sounding pleased, "you'd be the first."

He asked if any of my relatives had gone to Harvard, then told me I was to see another committee member in a short while.

During the wait, I felt deeply frustrated. When he reports to the committee, I was thinking, they're not going to quiz him on how much I know about the politics of Biafra. They're extremely unlikely to care about what I know of transplants and grafts. The relevant question is: How would a person who is blind but otherwise qualified deal with medicine, and learning medicine? And he hadn't asked me a thing to help answer that question.

The second man opened more bluntly and relevantly: "We try to get variety into each year's class. We're interested in you but are concerned about your not being able to see."

In discussing that, I remarked that Harvard's applications asked the candidate to list publications, and that I hadn't published anything.

"That's not the issue," he quickly assured me. "If we wanted all Ph.D. types, we'd find them. Your grades are adequate. The issue is whether you can be a doctor." He pointed out that I couldn't do surgery and couldn't look through a microscope.

I replied that psychiatrists do not perform surgery and that a few years into their careers most psychiatrists have no doubt lost their competency to tell one microbe from another. A psychiatrist, like any doctor, I said, must be able to discuss and read about surgery and microorganisms intelligently, and there was no reason I couldn't do that as well as anyone else.

I left Boston unable to tell Dad, or myself, anything about what kind of impression I made.

January and February brought cold turndowns from four more universities, leaving four possibilities out of the original ten: the crack in the door at Harvard; the Medical College of Pennsylvania; Temple; and the interview-despite-a-turndown at Yale.

Dad decided we'd drive the 160 miles or so to New

Haven for the Yale interview. That enabled Cheri to come with us.

"Whatever you do, Dave," Mom urged me repeatedly, "remember that they've practically promised to accept you in clinical psychology. Don't blow that by telling them to jump in the river if they insist they won't accept you for medical school."

She knew me well. It was good advice, and I promised.

The group I met from Yale's admissions committee was the most solemn group of doctors I'd ever encountered. I doubt that the guys bending over me to repair my retinas were more grave. We pulled and tugged for an hour over whether it was possible for a blind student to learn what they had to teach. ("Pulled and tugged" sounds like it was an evenly matched contest; it wasn't.) I pulled out every argument, every jab, every phrase and sentence that ever seemed to hit home in any interview, or even any parlor conversation I'd ever had. They didn't budge. I had no sense that they were listening, weighing, considering. One or another would keep saying, "Why don't you come here and go into clinical psychology?" One doctor maneuvered: "*Then* if things work out, maybe you could transfer into medical school."

I heard my mother's voice say, "Don't alienate them. Don't blow it." Just as easily as asking someone to pass the butter, I replied, "Why don't I start in medical school, then, if things don't work out, I could transfer to clinical psychology?"

"No, no, it won't work."

Meanwhile, out in an anteroom, I was soon to learn, a senior medical student joined Cheri and Dad, apparently assigned as a civic duty to take me to lunch after the interview. As Cheri relates it, the fellow sat down wordlessly, with an air of burden and boredom. He flipped through a newspaper, searching for something worthy of his attention, not finding it. Finally he deigned to inquire, "Related to that guy in there?"

"Yes, we're his father and fiancée."

Silence. Then, like fingering some unpleasant, unidentified goo: "He wants to go to medical school and there's something about his not being able to see?"

"Yes, that's right."

He put it a little more directly, more disdainfully: "He's *blind?*"

"Yes, that's right."

Silence. Then the fellow ventured again, "What's he able to do?"

"He's able to do a few things," Dad said.

For the first time the fellow showed a faint, distant trace of offering to be informative: "You know, medical school is very tough."

Dad took the news with equilibrium. "Yes, I know," he said.

I was not let in on the treat of that rarefied Ivy League discourse until later. But at lunch with my escort (Dad and Cheri betook themselves elsewhere), he lost no time in declaring where he was at.

"I just can't see how you'd do it," he volunteered. (Who asked him?) "I just can't imagine . . ."

My blood started to hiss the approach of boiling. All morning I'd kept myself strapped down, restraining myself from scalding that smug admissions committee. After enduring lunch with this idiot, I had to see Dr. Fredrick C. Redlich, dean of the medical school. Hopeless as my case was, there was yet a faint ray of hope: Redlich was a psychiatrist. If I could make him agree, no matter how reluctantly, that, yes, I could be a psychiatrist, that might be the last hairline crack that might enable me to pry the door open again. Also I had to see Dr. Ken Keniston, a psychologist of national reputation. The important appointment was ahead of me, with Redlich. The worst thing I could do before seeing him was to blow my control now by smashing down on this young idiot.

"You have to keep in mind," the senior medical student

intoned, "that if you were admitted, which I doubt you could be, you'd be taking a place, in a class of fixed size, that would otherwise go to someone who could see, and who could take much better advantage of a Yale education." I knew I was not going to be able to hold it. "And even if you did get through medical school, and I don't see how you could, you'd never be 'M.D.' like anyone else; you'd always be 'M.D., Blind.'"

That did it. Sorry, Mom.

"Now you listen to me for a minute," I said furiously. "I know I'll always be 'M.D., Blind.' But every doctor is M.D. Something, no matter who he is. Some are 'M.D., Overspecialized,' or 'M.D., Uncommunicative,' or 'M.D., Asocial,' or 'M.D., Narrow-minded,' or 'M.D., Fundamentally Stupid.' And I'm sick and tired of hearing about that guy whose place I'm going to take. I am qualified for this school. I'll match my college grades against yours. If I don't get in, that guy is taking *my* place. Remember that. I have earned my position in this school, and they're going to give it to somebody else."

I don't remember what else I said. All I remember is this guy saying sullenly, almost inaudibly, "You know, I think you might have a point." I was sure I hadn't convinced him of anything, but that he just wanted to get out of there.

I didn't feel scared about what I'd done. I didn't feel remorse for tromping on Mom's advice, even knowing she was right. I felt good. It was stupid to have sat there across from that self-satisfied, supercilious tribunal of the admissions committee and just let them walk barefoot all over me. I had earned the privilege of a little steaming and hollering. The hell with Redlich, I decided. I'm going to blast him. If that ruins their offer of clinical psych, let *them* worry about it. They've said what they think. I'm going to say what I think.

When I was shown into Redlich's office, he greeted me

quietly, as though his mind were elsewhere. The gentle sound of a page turning told me he was probably going over my application. Finally he said in slow, Vienna-shaped syllables, "Well, I think you present us with a very interesting prospect."

That just knocked my balls off.

Was he giving me the same runaround as his committee, but with a nice, soft, psychiatric cushion? Or did I catch a faint hint of challenge and adventure in that most overused and uninteresting of academic comments, "interesting"? He drew me out on what had become my hard-sell sales pitch, which apparently was corroborated by his own experience: that a psychiatrist needs a good understanding of the broad field of medicine, but does not have to prove his capacity to practice all its specialties. He kept saying, like lovely strokes on the back of my neck, "Of course, of course."

Did he meant it? Or was he slipping me a verbal tranquilizer? Finally he said, "Let's see what we can do about it. I can't promise you anything. Yes, I'm dean of this medical school, but that doesn't mean I have total say. I'm going to fight hard for you because I like you and I think you know what you're doing."

(An odd aftermath was that, for the rest of my final Gettysburg semester, my psychology course turned repeatedly to the work of the famous Dr. Fredrick Redlich. I'd not heard of him before and had no idea how revered a man had promised to go to bat for me.)

Within three weeks the letter I couldn't wait to get arrived from Yale. It said they had reevaluated my application after the initial decision to turn me down—and decided again to turn me down. At about the same time, Harvard, too, sent its regrets. The following June, Uncle Chill attended the Yale medical school reunion, made a point of looking up Dr. Redlich and introduced himself as my uncle. With Viennese gentleness, Redlich told him (if

I'm to believe Uncle Chill), "Those sons of bitches wouldn't listen to me."

The whole game would have now been down to the last do-or-die roll of the dice—specifically, Temple—if not for that last-minute suggestion by Dr. Schroeder's friend that I apply to Medical College of Pennsylvania, or "Women's." Temple had been so silent that right after Christmas vacation I had put in a call to make sure my application had been received. To my astonishment, Dr. Brigham, the associate dean, got on the phone himself and said, "Yes, everything is in order and we haven't forgotten you. In fact, you are very much under consideration." So the interview the previous year hadn't gone so badly after all.

Almost immediately after receiving my late application, someone from MCP called to suggest, "Why don't you come down for your interview Monday?" By God, they were really interested in me.

I was to see two admissions committee members, a woman who taught anatomy and bore my surname (I loved the sound of it: Doctor Hartman) and a Dr. Snow, a psychiatrist. I felt it went well. If anything discouraged me about the visit, it was Dr. Snow's mentioning that MCP had a special program that awarded a Ph.D. in psychiatry. I had never heard of a nonmedical degree in psychiatry, and still have no idea just what it is. My best guess is that it's essentially a clinical psychology program with extra emphasis on medical background.

Before the next day was over, I was to struggle through an obstacle course of ten interviews in two days. One interviewer seemed troubled by the weakest of my test scores —375 for verbal skill. "That disturbs me," said this doctor, "because you're going into psychiatry and in that specialty you're going to need a good vocabulary."

That thought has struck my funny bone every time I've heard it—and this was neither the first nor the last time I was to hear it. It mostly tells me how much many doctors misunderstand what goes on in psychiatry. The whole object is to lead people into seeing their own lives more lucidly, and I become increasingly convinced that a test of whether a perception is clear is whether it can be stated in extremely simple, unambiguous words. In the psychiatric residency I am serving as I write this, I meet a lot of people who bring their severe problems to a hospital clinic, usually because they're poor. Yes, sometimes I have trouble understanding them; sometimes I have to struggle to grasp what their words really mean. But it's not because their vocabularies are too large. Anyhow, my unsophisticated vocabulary had not done me in at Gettysburg, had not prevented a record of almost straight "A"s in science. And, as things turned out, it was not to be my downfall in medical school.

Temple hadn't even called me yet for my regular interview. That seemed a negative sign, a sign that in the end, they'd turn me down like the rest. So MCP was my lifeline.

Early in March the call from Temple finally came. The man I was to see was Dr. Joseph Baum, a pathologist. Right off, I liked the reasons he gave for why he was chosen to talk to me. He said that, while I was not headed toward internal medicine, I would need to understand it thoroughly. Pathology, the study of the nature of disease and changes in the body caused by disease, is a kind of halfway house between clinical medicine and basic sciences. He wanted to explore whether blindness would impair my understanding of biological processes.

He asked me to describe what a liver cell looked like. I replied that I visualized a liver cell as resembling a drop of water. The center of the area looked darker than the rest, and that was the nucleus. The lighter area around it was the cytoplasm. On closer examination through a highly powerful microscope with staining, one might possibly see a still darker area inside the nucleus. That would be an area of concentration of RNA, which helps make protein. I was unprepared for the question, and told him I wasn't sure about some of the details.

He replied, "I'm not trying to quiz you. At the moment, I'm not interested in whether you're factually right or wrong. I just want to understand your conception of what goes on, how you form conceptions."

Among other questions, he asked how I constructed a DNA molecule in my mind. I told him. But all his questions added up to a single, fundamental one: What does a person need to *conceptualize* if he's to be a doctor? And could I do it?

Next, Dr. Baum said something that told me this interview was curtains. He began saying, "You understand that we've had to worry over the problem that, no matter how impressed with you we are, you would be a special-risk student. If we give you a place in the freshman class, we're taking that place away from someone who doesn't . . ."

All the brightness he had lit by his brilliant line of questioning went dark. Another door slammed. In trying to pay attention, I realized that, along with the all-too-familiar phrases, he was saying something absolutely startling.

". . . can't in good conscience . . . deny a place . . . a sighted person who's earned it. But several of us, especially Dr. Brigham"—the associate dean who seemed so reserved and questioning in my preinterview months earlier—"have felt that *you* shouldn't be denied a place if *you've* earned it. How do we resolve that dilemma?

"Well, we've thought of one possible way to resolve it, but we have to give it more thought. Our freshman class has a hundred and eighty places. If we take you in, there are only a hundred and seventy-nine for students without your risk. Perhaps that *is* unfair to the hundred and eightieth, whoever he or she is out there. So someone, I believe it was Dr. Brigham, raised the question of why the incoming freshman class could not have a hundred and eighty-*one* places."

It was as though he had simply stated that the admissions committee had found a cure for cancer, though he added, "But we have to think about it further."

Spring came, bringing excitement and confusion. Cheri and I picked out her ring. Wayne, in his first year of osteopathic school, got married and I was best man. A most festive day, but a pervasively sad one, knowing that my best friend was leaving my life. Most confusing of all, all my friends were bubbling with anticipation of what they'd be doing the following year—and I alone still didn't know. Early in April I'd have to take entrance exams to confirm my eligibility for graduate school—specifically for clinical psychology, my fallback, if medical school didn't pan out. This was a long exam, about six hours.

On the night before the exam—a Friday night—Cheri and I were about to leave for a spaghetti dinner at a friend's when the phone rang. It was Dad. His voice was a little deeper than usual.

"Dave, I just got a call from Dr. Hartman at Women's, I mean at MCP, and—Dave—they've decided they're not going to accept you."

I felt the ground crack and tear under me. What Dad said was unbelievable. I just knew that MCP was going to accept me. I couldn't, wouldn't, believe it.

"What reason did they give?" I managed to ask.

"They gave no reason, Dave. But they said you'd be able to get into their Ph.D. program in psychiatry."

Maybe I could take that and somehow slip over into medical school. But they turned me down. If they did, Temple surely would. No school of the ten I'd talked to was as receptive to making an experiment of me as MCP.

This was the crushing blow that for year after year after year I'd never permitted myself to imagine would come. I hung up the phone and sat on my bed. As long as I could remember, my stubbornness had always saved me. My parents saying I couldn't have something never really meant no. There was always a way. But now there was no way. Every plan, every dream, was crushed and gone. The surface of the world was all mush, no place to stand without sinking.

Cheri and I found ourselves crying on each other. I felt a stupid fool, a little kid playing a game of getting into medical school, playing it so convincingly that now everybody was used up and exhausted, all their time wasted, and there was nothing to show for it but my foolishness and stupidity.

I'd have to face Mom, who had been right all the time. I'd have to face everyone I knew at Gettsyburg: Don Johnson, who had just been accepted for dental school; others who'd made it into medical school; and professors Cavaliere and Schroeder and the others whom I'd conned into my game, and tell them all that it—well, it just didn't work out, ha ha.

But there was no reason I had to go through the torture of telling friends right this minute at a spaghetti dinner. Cheri and I went to a restaurant called the Pub. We ordered steaks that we couldn't afford.

Despite a crippling feeling of depression, I had to write a paper for a course in theology and literature. I chose to write it on Ernest Hemingway's novel *The Old Man and the Sea*. The story, of course, is about an old fisherman in an old boat who finds himself doing battle with the most tremendous fish he's ever challenged. For three agonizing days and nights he fights it, finally subduing it and tying it to the side of his creaking boat, but by the time he floats the mighty beast back to shore, it's all been devoured by sharks. At the end, exhausted, the old man is left not with a fish, but simply his experience of it.

I wrote in my paper that the old man did not lose by the effort that went wrong, but grew, gained, indeed won by committing himself to the effort, regardless of its outcome. The process of the old man's risking and striving for success was itself a success, far more meaningful than simply bringing the fish home.

Doing that paper was an engrossing emotional experience. My failed attempt to get into medical school was not wasted, not a failure at all. What had I lost? I'd enjoyed the involvement and commitment of shooting toward a goal—which, like pursuing that fish, was more rewarding than achieving the goal itself. I'm sure I learned more from my courses, and got better grades, than I would have if that difficult goal had not motivated me. I could now choose a career in clinical psychology with virtually no doubt of acceptance into a fine school, which might not have been the case had I not geared up for medical school. Even losing was winning. (And as a final plus, that paper on *The Old Man and the Sea* got an "A.")

I so convinced myself of that philosophy that, a few days after the MCP rejection, when Al Schroeder invited me to the Pub for consolation and beer, I heard myself saying that the experience of trying and losing would probably serve my life—and, in a way, my career—better than trying and succeeding. My mind was made up, I told him; I wanted to work with disabled people as a psychologist now that it was clear I would not be a psychiatrist. I now knew something about losing, about hopelessness, about real disability, that I had not previously known. Schroeder waited, quizzically. I explained that blindness had never been a real disability to me; whatever I wanted to do, I could always find a way. But as a result I never really had to comprehend the terrible psychological chains of feeling disabled. And I told Schroeder that only now, for the first time, when I was denied something flat out because I was blind—something I wanted, something I worked for, something I believe I earned—only now when my blindness had cost me the career I wanted, did I truly understand frustration, the prison of disability.

I was rationalizing like crazy, getting caught up in my own dramatic spell. Yet as I look back, it was a damned interesting rationalization. I could convince myself of it again.

One evening toward the end of May, two days before final exams, Cheri and I had the $1 student special at the Lamp Post after a long, tedious day of studying separately. After dinner, she said she had to cram through some statistical work in the computer room. Cheri ran through a downpour to her destination, and I tapped my way to my dorm, arriving waterlogged.

I remember the moment. I was standing in the doorway of two friends, Dave Fritchman and Tom Beers, when the phone rang down the hall. Phones in dorms ring long because everyone hearing them figures someone else will answer. After half a dozen rings I ambled over. Someone picked it up before I got there and said, "It's for you, Dave."

I took it. "Hello?"

"Hello-lo, Dave-ave?" Two separate voices, both Mom's and Dad's. Then Dad's voice alone, sounding grave, gravelly, artificially deep as though suppressing something, said, "Dave, your sister has something to tell you."

My God, something's happened to Bobbie, something disastrous.

Bobbie picked up a third phone. Mom must be upstairs. Dad's in his basement darkroom. Bobbie, the one in trouble, is in the kitchen.

"Dave," Bobbie began shakily, "you've been accepted at Temple."

I couldn't believe what I'd heard. I'm positive I asked her to say it again, although maybe I just played back the words in my head: "You've been accepted at Temple."

There is no way, simply no way, I can describe accurately the rush of feelings, thoughts, fulfillments, and flashes of white-hot light that filled my head in an instant, except to try to explain the feeling of my life suddenly transforming from "God, what am I going to do next year?" to "It's happened—*I'm going to be a doctor.*"

Colors ignited in my head. I always picture the seasons as colors and the changing of the seasons as a kind of circle of color. Fall—the start of the school year—is gray mixed with brownish. Winter is black and silvery. I keep hearing about spring being bright green. I see it as a pink-yellow-ish, but mainly just bright. Summer is warm and yellow orange. When Bobbie said the news the second time, the brownish gray of the coming September just exploded, the sky in my head blazing with big red words, MEDICAL SCHOOL.

Another wave of that rush was the thrill of feeling that, in making this crazy dream come true, I'd broken a barrier, done something nobody in my lifetime had done. And still another wave, one I'm a little less proud to admit: My financial future suddenly is secure; I'll never again be a blind beggar trying to find a way to make a living, pleading with someone to hire me, waiting while he wonders whether I can do anything. The news from Bobbie, which still seemed unreal and I asked her to repeat it yet again, suddenly meant that I'd have a job, that I'd have a job for the rest of my life.

I didn't have enough pockets to contain the joy, and it spilled all over. I had to find Cheri. I had to tell her. Immediately. I couldn't tell anyone until I told Cheri. I slipped on a summer jacket, grabbed my collapsible white cane, and dashed outside into a terrific downpour that made a soaking dishrag out of my jacket. Her dorm was on the opposite end of the campus. I had to cross two streets, but not busy ones. Classes having just ended that afternoon, I had no sense of where she'd be. I hadn't thought of phoning her dorm. I just wanted to see her.

Her room was empty. I ran—actually, walked as fast as I could, which feels like running—to the library, halfway back to my dorm. In the library I had to walk around —around the catalog files, around the reading rooms—so that Cheri could see me if she was there.

"Hey, Dave, you look like a raggedy mop." It was Bill Dundon, one of my closest dorm friends.

"I've got to find Cheri. Do you see her?"

"Is something wrong?"

"No, nothing's wrong. I can't tell you, but it's really important."

That was enough for Bill. He was off to every room and corner of the library, looking. Soon he returned, sounding distressed. "I can't find her."

"Bill, I can't have you running all over for me without telling you. I got into Temple."

That library never heard such a whoop. While he was hugging and pummeling me, I suddenly remembered. She'd said she was going to the computer room. I grabbed Bill's elbow and we raced to the basement of the Gladfelter Building, one of the biggest and oldest on campus, with an imposing tower that I always see when someone says Gladfelter. In the basement I called her out of the room, shut the door on the cushioned whirring of the computer, tried to think of a dramatic sentence, and blurted out, "Cheri, I got accepted at Temple."

She threw herself at me and collapsed into tears. Right in that quiet corridor, Bill mumbled something and I heard him go away. He felt he shouldn't be there.

We went to my room, and I said, "Cheri, I have this

nagging fear that maybe I just misheard the whole thing."
I phoned my parents back. Mom said, "Yes, Dave, you've
been accepted."

I called Cavaliere and Schroeder, and one of them asked,
"When can we meet you at the Pub?"

"Half an hour."

"Fine. We'll be there."

They told me they were buying, and I ordered rusty
nails, a concoction composed of scotch and Drambuie. The
four of us had the best party I've ever been at. After two
rusty nails, you don't remember anything. I had three, so
there's nothing more I can tell about it. I was told the next
day—just before my final exams, which somehow I got
myself to—that Cavaliere took us all home for recuperative
coffee. But you couldn't prove it by me.

Properly I should end this chapter telling about my
graduation. But nice as it was, it couldn't match getting
accepted at Temple in the rain and that night at the Pub.
So take my word for it: I graduated, and it felt good.

❧❧ 13 ❧❧

A Freshman
on Broad Street

When something is anticipated long and intensely, as starting medical school was for me, the high and low points of the experience are always surprising, never what you expected.

The most dazzling experience of my first week, totally unimagined in advance, was a press conference. And the most horrifying was my introduction to the revolving door. I'd never had to deal with revolving doors, at least not alone, and now I faced them at the entrances to the medical school, the hospital, and my dorm.

A revolving door that's standing still, of course, is no problem. But one spinning busily all the time with people hurrying in and out is quite another matter. My parents spent a full hour my first day helping me figure out how I could manage those doors with confidence and without breaking my arm off. (It took almost that full hour to discover that the rubber flap bordering the door is quite wide and that arm-breaking is highly improbable.) I finally devised a choreography: Stick hand out, let rubber flap whack fingers, pull hand back quickly, let one section go by, and jump into the next. If the flap whacked my hand slowly, I might just jump into the first section.

Of course, that system was fine for getting *me in*, but wasn't so hot for allowing a previous occupant of that section to get out. I was meeting an awful lot of people. So I figured out a quick left-hand motion for testing whether someone was making a getaway before I plunged. That left-hand jab is accompanied by a slight tilting forward of the head, on the theory that, if the hand misinforms me, it's his bloody nose or mine.

A secondary problem was getting used to elevators. Even though those doors automatically reopen when they're obstructed, it's surprising and scary to get thumped in their squeeze. I also had to be able to locate the right button for my floor. In our dorm we had the heat-sensitive kind of button system—just the touch of your finger lights it up and instructs the mechanism. I could find the proper little square for my floor by running my finger up the rim of the squares so as not to light up the whole board. But if I wanted to screw a fellow student, I'd play dumb and start counting up to, say, eleven, touching them all. Sometimes I'd generously ask him *his* floor, then go eentsy-weentsy spider up to eight or thirteen while the poor guy peed in his pants, not wanting to bawl out an unfortunate blind guy. School does have its better moments.

I put up a bulletin-board notice asking for readers. The responses swamped me—about a dozen, enabling me to give tryouts and be selective. Most students were reluctant to accept the couple of bucks an hour I offered. Their feeling seemed to be, "If Temple can stick its neck out on this experiment, I want to help." Medical students are terribly pressed for time, but highly motivated to help others. Maybe that's what makes them want to be doctors.

I made some good friends among my readers, and most memorable was Marion Moses. When she entered medical school with me, she was thirty-six, a fact that made her acceptance by the admissions committee almost as difficult as mine. Perhaps that made her identify with me. A feminist, assertive, and extremely bright, Marion had been a nurse in California and, searching for an avenue of deeper commitment, went to work for Cesar Chavez, the crusading union organizer of migratory farm workers. But her limited skills as a nurse frustrated her, and she determined to become a doctor. I've never met anyone more involved in more things, yet a knowledgeable and hardworking student—and still she found time to read for me. Her medical knowledge and natural efficiency were invaluable. She'd scan page after page of material, knowing I had to be selective about my reading, and she'd say, "Dave, this paragraph's important, this section's important, this is important. The rest is bullshit." She was not only blunt, but always accurate about what I needed to know and what was a waste of time.

One big difference between medical school and any other kind of schooling I'd ever had was that for a period of weeks we'd concentrate almost exclusively, all day, every day, on a single subject area. Our freshman year began with ten weeks of anatomy—gross anatomy, microscopic anatomy, and developmental anatomy. In gross anatomy I became a member of a four-student team. Perhaps I should say a five-person team. The fifth member was relatively inactive, although central to our work. He was dead. We called him Duke.

To save our time, and probably to prevent an awful mess at the hands of inexperienced freshmen, the school paid upperclassmen to cut open and lay back the skins and outer layers of our cadavers. So there was Duke, letting it all hang out. The thought of fondling his insides was repulsive and terrifying, but our brilliant professor, Carson Schneck, who held a Ph.D. in anatomy as well as an M.D., had ways of knocking those fears and resistance right out of us. He'd announce an exam in a very few days: "You'll have to know exactly where all those nerves come from and where they go. It'll all be on the exam, and if you don't pass it, you can't go on." He'd tell us to do this, feel that, learn this, be able to describe that. Rapidly. Under the pressure he cleverly and skillfully created, we were all— and no freshman was anything less than terrified—forced to forget our emotional reactions and get down to learning.

I fingered every running inch of a skeleton that dangled in our lab, every bend, every depression, every crevice of every bone. Then I'd go back to Duke and find which nerves, which muscles, connected with the bone in each crevice, following those muscles and nerves to their opposite terminals. I'd feel the superior and inferior areas of the scapula along my own shoulder, and my own muscle structures. After a short while, running my fingers along the stringy gristle of Duke's nervous system was no more strange than fingering pickled beets. That comparison is more apt than it may appear. The nerves and muscles in a cadaver don't feel human; they don't suggest life. They feel pickled.

Another thing I did was astonishingly clarifying. In the anatomy course, we'd have to inject, say, the shoulder of a hospital patient, or students would inject one another. Later that evening, or in a day or two, I'd examine Duke's shoulder to feel exactly what the needle penetrated. A needle doesn't just disappear below the skin, it goes *through* stuff. I wanted to know what it goes through. Duke eventually dispelled the fearsome question with which I'd begun: Can I really learn anatomy without seeing what I'm examining?

One day in a kind of oral preexam, Dr. Schneck asked me to show him a certain nerve in Duke's brachial plexus. I touched the clavicle, a small bone connecting the shoulderblade with the breastbone, then ran my finger beneath it along a major nerve structure branching from the spinal cord and spreading into the arm. I fingered the nerve he named.

"No, I don't believe that's right, Dave."

It had to be right. Duke had a textbook brachial plexus. Was Dr. Schneck mistaken in seeing what I pointed out, or was he putting me on, challenging me to hold my ground? "I really believe it is," I said.

To this day I don't know why Dr. Schneck first contradicted me, but I do remember the glow I felt when he patted my shoulder and said, "You're right."

Passing that anatomy course was important beyond imagining. Not only because it was the first part of the first year, but because I knew I couldn't bear repeating ten weeks of that mixed odor of formaldehyde and decay.

There was only one manner of dealing with Duke that I never got used to: feeling his face and his hands. There is something about the face and the hands that makes them unmistakable evidences of personhood, haunting reminders of life.

Anatomy involves the study of X rays—learning to read X rays, and being tested on the reading of X rays. Obviously, there is no way I can read an X ray. I can understand what's on an X ray, the medical and surgical significance of what someone might see there, but someone's got to tell me what's on it. No way I can read it.

So that gave us our first testing problem. The professors decided there was no point in "testing" me on what I couldn't do and would never be called upon in practice to do. So if an anatomy exam had 100 questions, and five required reading and interpreting X rays, I would be graded as though the exam had 95 questions. Each correct answer to those 95 questions was worth a little more than to other students.

I thought that method was fair and proper—partly. Fairness also required that if I was to earn the same medical degree as everyone else, I had to pass an exam on equal terms with everyone else. So while they graded me their way on the few exams where certain questions were exempted, I always figured out what my grade would have been if those questions had not been exempted and I'd lost points for those questions going unanswered. I can report that during my years of medical school I never came close to a failing grade in an exam, even counting exempted questions as wrongly answered. In every major exam I can remember, my grades were in the upper half of the class, often in the top quarter.

I prepared for every exam convinced that I had a fifty-fifty chance of failing it, especially that first one in anatomy. As at Gettysburg, I'd live on two hours of sleep for each of several nights before the exam. I'd be irritable, scared, diarrhetic, certain I was developing an ulcer. In college, my worry was that I wouldn't get an "A," therefore wouldn't get into medical school. Now, in medical school, my worry was that I wouldn't pass. It was a heady thrill, coming out of that first major exam with, as best I recall, a 90. Heady, all right—but no help at all in reducing my anxieties over the next exam, or the one after that, or after that. The next one was always the first one I was going to fail.

Anatomy was followed by courses in histology and biochemistry, which, while high-pressure, presented no special problems. Temple professors quickly and readily adapted to my use of raised-line drawings and models in place of peering through a microscope. Indeed one of the surprises was that medical school, while always high-pressure, was essentially simple, almost all pure memory. Oh, God, how everyone of us would weary of memorizing. Some days, especially toward the end of the week, you'd feel you just couldn't find room in your head to stuff another fact, another symptom, the name of another drug.

Classes began at eight in the morning and we sat there

and got lectured at until noon, with periodic ten-minute breaks. Everybody would get sleepy, but I developed a reputation as the sleepiest. Professors tolerated sleepers. These were not classes of, say, thirty, as in high school, but vast congregations of 180 or so. Each class would seek out its best note taker, and employ him at an hourly rate to draw up an outline of each lecture. These outlines would be mimeographed overnight and distributed next morning. I always subscribed to that service, at about $30 a year, then I'd cadge somebody to read the outline to me before tucking it away. Amazing how much you can learn from a concise outline of a three-hour lecture that put you to sleep with its dreary detail.

Not trusting those subscription outlines entirely, however, I'd whisper notes into my tape recorder. If a lecture seemed particularly important or rich in useful detail, I'd tape the whole thing. Unfortunately, the knowledge that the slow-spinning reels of my machine were capturing the professor's wisdom would itself lull me to sleep. The end of the tape cassette would cause the recorder to emit a compelling, tinny *beeeeep* that would startle me out of my sleep, which made everybody around me laugh. One enterprising bastard taped—on his machine—the beep of my machine. When he saw me doze he'd slip his machine behind my seat and jar me awake with his tape of my beep. I'd leap up, frantically eject my cassette, flip it over, and confidently slide back to slumber, wondering what everyone thought was so funny.

There's an old med school wisecrack that a psychiatrist is someone whose mother wanted him to be a doctor, but who can't stand the sight of blood. What makes the namby-pambies pass out, actually, is not usually blood but shocking intimacy with the innards of a living body. Med students can't be certain they can cross that great divide until they've done it.

My own crossing occurred one day, unexpectedly, in physiology lab, and I'm not sure I can honestly claim to have made it successfully, since I did pass out.

It's customary in a certain phase of physiology lab to gas a dog or two into unconsciousness, enabling students to inject it with varieties of fluids and test the resultant changes in heartbeat, blood pressure, and whatnot, as well as to conduct other examinations and even perform surgery.

On this particular day a student more advanced than I, a most helpful fellow who often kept an eye out to make sure I didn't unnecessarily miss anything, called to me and said, "Dave, feel this dog I've got here." The dog's neck was open, with tubes coming out to insure it could breathe. "You ought to feel this. Push the neck tissues aside and get your fingers down to the trachea and feel that big artery. Feel that fat vessel? That's the carotid artery that's feeding the brain. Leave your finger there and you'll feel the warm air pumping in and out."

I felt relieved when a moment later he suggested I get my fingers out of the dog and feel the external plastic breathing tube, also pumping rhythmically, so I could sense the connection between the breathing and the supply of oxygen to the dog's brain. While fascinated by the physiological drama and my friend's enthusiasm, I was also profoundly shaky from poking the organs and vessels of that dog. I wanted—*needed*—to sit down. While air was pumping into the dog's brain, my blood was leaving mine. I tried to remember that a good, red-blooded male doesn't faint. The next thing I knew I was in another room with my feet up and head down, feeling the breath and hearing the close voice of my professor, "Are you okay? Did you have enough for breakfast?"

"No," I lied instinctively, "I didn't have *any* breakfast."

Fooling around with Duke had never done this to me. Being cold, a cadaver feels plastic, unreal. But the warm, pulsating, sticky insides of this dog were life itself.

That was the first and last time I ever felt that way. In

a few days I was overcome with an urge to perform surgery on a dog—a tracheotomy. I had this unnerving fantasy of sitting at a grand dinner one night when one of the guests swallows wrong and starts to choke, and another guest yells, "Is there a doctor in the house?" and still another shouts triumphantly, "Yes, Dr. Hartman is here!" Then I have to say, "Sorry, I was exempted from surgery and never performed a tracheotomy. We'll just have to let the fellow die." (Not till later did I learn that a dog tracheotomy is different from a human tracheotomy.)

That same graduate student eagerly volunteered to work with me. Under his coaching I slit the dog's throat. He'd say, "There's a blood vessel near the top of the neck . . . now go to the side . . . do this . . . do that. . . ."

I did the whole thing, and one thing I learned was that slitting and stretching the skin of a dog turned me off. I decided then and there I was not cut out to be a surgeon. But you'd never know it from the neat way I punctured, shafted, and patched up that animal.

Getting through that first year of medical school was a double triumph. First, just getting through (and, as it turned out, with above average grades) confirmed that I might survive the rest of it. Second, Cheri simultaneously got her diploma at Gettysburg, and we had our wedding.

Considering how totally enjoyable I found our wedding day, I was shocked that almost everyone else seemed teary-eyed. About a hundred relatives and friends packed the Elks Club at Belmar, New Jersey, near the home of Cheri's mother. From Gettysburg came Bill Dundon, Fred Wright, Don Johnson, and other friends. Cheri's roommate, Nancy Bowker, and Wayne (my best man) played guitars and sang Mary Travers's "Follow Me" and "The Song Is Love." Our Gettysburg chaplain, Rev. John Vannorsdall, who has since become the chaplain at Yale, performed the ceremony. He reflected our hopes and feelings exactly when he stressed in his talk that, although married and sharing a home and family, we would not become one through fusion, neither of us living to serve the other; we would remain separate people, living separate lives as professionals and as persons, each having a separate impact on the world. That was our ambition and has since become the theme of our marriage.

Cheri enrolled at Temple for graduate work in educational psychology and, at this writing, is close to earning her Ph.D. Like mine, it is a demanding course of study. We had no intention of expecting her to make a career of sacrificing to my career. Sure, we might divide responsibilities in ways that sighted couples might not. I help with the housework. Obviously, she does all the driving. She balances the checkbook. Sometimes she'll retype a letter that I've made a mess of. Just as I've asked some friends at school to do, when she has time she might read to me. But the needs of her career claim the priority on her time.

Now that I've made that perfectly clear, let me tell you that it wasn't always that simple and easy. Anytime—in fact, every time—I tried to duck out of vacuuming or doing the dishes or cleaning the bathroom, Cheri was no easier on me than Bobbie had been. The problem of who cooks solved itself easily. At Gettysburg I did lots of cooking for myself, and my dormmates were amazed at my flawlessly distinguishing a can of spaghetti from a can of applesauce. Cheri's tummy, however, was not impressed with my cuisine. She'd survived, perhaps even been amused by, a Gettysburg hamburger or two, but now, faced with a steady diet of my culinary skills, she decided I cleaned the bathroom better.

During the first year of our marriage we discussed having children someday, after my training was over. The special question for us, of course, was the risk of blindness in our children and how we felt about that risk. My tendency to seriously defective eyes has an extremely small likelihood of being inherited, and Cheri says she'd far sooner assume the very low risk of having a sightless child than having no children at all. I think I draw the line at the prospect of two or three blind children. That would enslave a mother who has as many ambitions of her own as Cheri has.

14

Getting Through

In the early pages of this story, I mentioned the pediatrician who was too blind to detect that something was wrong with my eyes, so instead scolded my mother for bringing me up poorly. In the summer between my freshman and sophomore years of medical school, I met a more dramatic illustration that functioning eyes do not a good doctor make.

The guy I'm thinking of was a successful and prominent physician in an affiliated hospital. For the summer I took a job with a medical research project on the psychiatric aspects of death and dying. The psychiatrist directing the project, not having terminal patients within his own practice, assigned me to the aforementioned physician, whom I'll call Dr. Graves. He specialized in patients who had cancer.

He soon struck me as strange. I asked his permission to stand in on his surgery sometime, perhaps with another medical student who might tell me what was going on. People observe surgery all the time. "Oh, my God, no," he replied, thunderstruck. "That would be terrible, a blind person in there. Oh, I'd be very nervous. I couldn't deal with it. The operating room is a very serious place."

What the hell did he think I was going to do, jog around the room, knocking things over? Still, refusing me was his privilege.

Then he instructed me to meet him next morning outside the operating room so he could tell me which of his patients I ought to interview. Being unfamiliar with that hospital, I asked where the operating room was. He replied, "Oh, I don't think I ought to make things too easy for you. You should find out yourself. I'll meet you there at ten."

The next morning, after our little conference, Dr. Graves blurted, "Now I realize, Dave, what bugs me about you." (I hadn't known I bugged him.) "Last night I was watching TV and they portrayed this blind child who upset me."

"Why?"

"The child was feeling something with his fingers while he was looking off somewhere toward the North Star. He wasn't facing what he was doing, wasn't looking at it. You face me when we talk, but you don't look at me. It would be much better if you tried to focus your eyes on me."

I didn't know what to tell him. But later, back at the office of my project director, an exuberant, jolly, robust psychiatrist who had felt to me like an instant old friend, I told of my encounter. I asked whether he, too, felt bugged by my lack of eye contact. I confessed that Dr. Graves had upset me and I felt guilty about my reaction.

My psychiatrist boss blew up. "Dave, you're crazy. I can't believe what I'm hearing you say. You need to get angry at this guy. From what you tell me, you're letting him worry you that it's something *you're* doing. You've *got* to get angry at him."

I guess that scolding freed me to accept that doctors aren't necessarily gods. And that I'm not the first seriously handicapped person to have made it past a medical school admissions committee.

In sophomore year we did our first physical examinations, three to four hours apiece, and wrote them up. The subjects of the exams were hospital patients, and naturally these exams by medical students did not substitute for, but were in addition to, full exams by residents or other qualified doctors. The patients, however, did not necessarily know that one examination was for their benefit and another was for the examiner's benefit.

I'm sure there's a moral issue involved, but I've thought about it a lot and cannot come up with a satisfactory answer. Do we have the right to take advantage of a patient this way just because he's in a university hospital? But an equally valid question is: How else are doctors to be trained? By totally respecting the privacy of patients—and depriving future doctors of basic experience, thus also endangering their future patients? Is it not a legitimate form of partial payment for a patient to have the benefits of a university hospital? I don't know. But I do know it's routinely done. And of course there's always the rationalization that the student might come up with a diagnostic discovery that his superiors missed. Hmmm.

In September 1974, the beginning of my third year of medical school, I chose as my first six-week rotation the first formal course I had in psychiatry. Normally a student requests rotations in more basic medical areas first—gynecology and obstetrics, internal medicine, neurology, and so forth. Psychiatry is usually left for the end, partly because some future doctors are uncomfortable talking with people and can't grasp the idea of talking and listening as a form of diagnosis and healing, partly because many of them don't see psychiatry as important to the specialty they plan to go into. In contrast, I couldn't wait to get a more serious taste of the specialty that attracted me most. Even in doing medical histories the previous year, what interested me most was not so much collecting facts as gaining patients' trust and making them emotionally comfortable, perhaps stimulating them into making connections between bits of their history that they had not previously realized.

Besides the usual crushing load of reading and lectures, the psychiatry rotation entailed once-a-week visits to a private psychiatric hospital and a community mental-health clinic. The best part of it, however, was doing my own psychiatric interviews with patients, under supervision.

The way we worked was that I (or any med student doing the psychiatric rotation) would interview a psychiatric clinic patient in a small, comfortable room, one wall of which was a one-way window. On the other side would sit my psychiatry professor or a psychiatry resident, and perhaps two or three psychiatry students like myself to learn from the instructor's comments on what I might be doing right or wrong. If my interview took some thoughtless turn, or if I muffed a good opportunity to help the patient make a breakthrough, a phone on my little table would ring. Presumably, the patient would think I was taking a routine office call, but actually it would be my professor calling to say, in effect, "For God's sake, Dave, you fool! . . ."

I still hear of people who express doubt that a blind person can be a good psychiatrist, because of all the visual clues—facial expressions, etc.—that he'd miss. I totally disagree. People who've had no contact with the field must imagine a shrink as someone who glares at a patient in the manner of a Scotland Yard inspector, beady-eyed and suspicious, picking up secrets of the patient's inner soul from the way he bites his nails.

The truth, of course, is that most of the "inspecting" has to be done by the patient, tripping himself up in his own delusions and self-deceits. Sure, a psychiatrist has to be highly observant, but not necessarily with his eye. After all, when a psychiatrist recommends that the patient lie down, the patient often moves out of the psychiatrist's line of vision. The most important thing, of course, is what the patient says. The way he says it may give important clues to how he feels about what he's saying. Does he suddenly stutter and hesitate? Does his voice quaver? Does he, in midsentence, forget what he was talking about? I can't help but notice if a person keeps tapping his finger on a table, or fidgets with an ashtray, or clears his throat often and unnecessarily, or laughs inappropriately. Those clues are not only as valuable as visual clues, they invariably accompany them.

Visual clues might reinforce the clues I hear, but they have just as much chance of confusing and distorting them. In a first interview with one of my patients, I picked up some weird vibes from him, yet felt reasonably comfortable and thought we could get somewhere. After the hour, however, my classmates on the other side of the one-way mirror complimented me on "covering up" my true feelings toward the patient. That cynical and twisted look on his face, they said, really stirred their hostility and suspicion. I didn't know what they were talking about.

At our next interview the patient volunteered to me that one of the main sources of his unbearable problem with other human beings was that there seemed to be some peculiar way he stared at other people, which he felt made them all hate him. He added that knowing I couldn't see him relaxed him. He could just be himself without worrying about whether his peculiar, and apparently unintended, stare put me off.

I'm not suggesting, because of this one unusual case, that being blind helps me be a better psychiatrist, but I don't think it has anything to do with being a poorer one.

Another ironic twist was a black patient who refused to

deal with me because I was white and she felt entitled to a black therapist. The irony, of course, was that the pigment of her skin, or, for that matter, my own, could scarcely have been of less influence in my dealing with her, since it was invisible to me.

From my psychiatry rotation I went directly into six weeks of obstetrics and gynecology. For the first few days I was in a fog, and finally realized that other students were ahead of me because most of them had just completed internal medicine. They'd been poking inside people's abdomens while I'd been poking inside their minds.

One reason the fog soon lifted was that one of my professors, an Indian surgeon, about four-foot-ten and Napoleonically strong-willed, consistently strove to make sure that my sightlessness did not prevent a full learning experience. He'd stand me by his side and have me stick my rubber-gloved hand into laid-open bellies, not only to follow his operation, usually a hysterectomy, but to get me on intimate terms with the gut, the stomach, the liver, all the machinery around.

One time he had me perform almost all of a D & E—dilation and evacuation—the trade name for a type of abortion. He inserted the vacuum tube into the uterus, but had me manipulate it, moving it up and down and around to suction out the conceptus—the fetus—and make sure all of it was out. I know this may make some people shudder, feeling that the patient was subjected to unfair risk beyond what she would experience with another supervised medical student. But like some other medical and surgical procedures, this one has to be performed "blind," since the critical organ and the procedure being performed on it is not available to the surgeon's vision. So why can't I be expected to perform it as competently as an equally trained sighted person?

That reminds me of the most curious occurrence during that six-week rotation. I was requested by a third-year resident, four years ahead of me, to do a history and physical on one of his ob-gyn patients. I appreciated his confidence and the opportunity. The exam went perfectly well, except for the routine breast exam. I reported on my sheet that I felt no breast tissue whatsoever, and suggested there might be a hormone problem.

My senior colleague asked if she might be tricking me. Never having heard this fellow of earnest but often plodding mind engage in the style of off-color banter peculiar to med students, I was surprised at his wisecrack, until I realized it wasn't a wisecrack. He meant it.

"What do you mean, tricking me?" I asked.

"Maybe she had you feeling her belly button," he replied.

I assured him that, even without staring at it, I could tell a nipple from a belly button. I almost voiced the question that flashed through my mind: "When you make love, do you have to turn the lights on?"

I remember one long, dreary night of hospital duty in the delivery room with Dick Heinz, who was superior company as well as a superior student. We filled the dragging hours with coarse fantasies. One of them was a "plan" that next time an about-to-be mother came racing in ahead of the arrival of her private doctor, I'd walk in, conspicuously rapping my cane on the marble floor, maybe an outstretched hand fumbling ahead of me, and announce, "Your doctor just called to say he can't make it, so I'm going to do the delivery. I can't see a damn thing, but that's all right, you just tell me what to do and I'll do it."

After we tired of wringing that dry, we fell serious and were soon engaged in a searching and intimate discussion of what we were experiencing as medical students. I found myself confessing to discouragement at how hard the going sometimes was, the amount of help I needed from guys who seemed to know more, how I always felt I was slowing others down, and the doubts that always haunted me that I might not be able to contribute enough to justify all this help I needed. I wondered if I should really be going through something less visual, like psychology, instead of medicine.

"Do you really feel that way?" Dick asked. I was sure he was going to pat my shoulder and encourage me to quit without feeling guilty.

"Sometimes," I admitted.

"So do I," he said. "I thought I was the only one. Maybe everybody around here feels that way, and everyone's afraid to say it."

As I observed the sweet shock of hearing this superior student match my confession, he added the topper: "But I'm surprised that *you* feel that way, Dave. You always look like you've got it all down pat and under control."

Thereafter, anytime I felt dangerously down, I'd pump another student—a star student, if possible—on his fears, and I'd feel better. Which was a good thing, because the beginning of every rotation during each of those two years in the hospital was a terror. Every time a new subject began I had to deal with new people—students and residents as well as professors with whom I hadn't worked before. I had to start from scratch, educating them about working with a blind person. I had to learn my way around physically, work with new equipment, in new routines, adapt to the lecturing styles of new instructors whose ways were probably too set to change for the needs of a student who couldn't see their charts and blackboards. The new start every six weeks drove me nuts and, as a consequence, I'd go home and drive Cheri nuts.

But I got through. Somehow I did, by God, get through, and with plenty to spare. And in June of 1976 at a ceremony I always knew—yet never quite believed—would happen, I accepted a parchment scroll that rechristened me David W. Hartman, M.D.

15

Looking Back

If people refuse to let me be their doctor because I'm blind, I still won't have to worry about earning a living. No indeed. I am a trained, skilled, kitchen-tested, certified basket weaver—probably almost as good as those destitute and illiterate natives of Bolivia or Nepal or Upper Volta or wherever it is that whole families scrounge their way through life weaving baskets.

Basket weaving was a required course at Overbrook in sixth and seventh grade. In midcourse I went to see the school administrator I thought was most intelligent. With school grades that ranked me as academically superior, I wanted to know why I had to waste my time taking basket weaving. With an air of not expecting me to understand cold, cruel reality as he did, he explained that if all else failed I could always fall back on earning my living as a basket weaver.

"Why can't we study electricity?" I asked. "I could always fall back on being an electrician."

"Because most of you won't be able to do electrical work. Basket weaving is much more practical if you need a job."

That offended me. The full reason it offended me hit home some years later in a talk with a friend of mine, a prizewinning writer in the field of education. He was telling me of a shocking experience he'd had writing about schools in urban ghettos in the early 1960s when educators were first discovering that children born and raised in extreme poverty are not like other children. Foundation and government money poured into ghetto schools to "help" those kids—the lion's share of the money going to retrain teachers. My friend heard well-meaning teachers, one after another, return from their courses wondering aloud, "But is it *fair* to lift the educational level of these poor kids too much, to take the risk of raising their hopes, qualifying them for better jobs, when there may turn out to be no jobs out there for them?" Translation: Wouldn't it be kinder, more humane, to keep these benighted kids dumb, unaware, spiritless, and impotent?

I do not know firsthand how widespread that attitude was—or is—in schools for the poor. But I suspect the attitude still lingers, perhaps dominates, among many teachers, as well as among many welfare workers and social-work helpers of every variety. I surmise that is so because I know, from my own frustrating experience, how cruelty-through-help has been inflicted on the blind by the "blind establishment," the vast structure of organizations—about 800 across the United States—professionally devoted to making life easier for people who can't see.

In criticizing the "blind establishment"—made up of sighted as well as blind helpers of the blind—I do not question anyone's purity of motive. But, for that matter, I don't question Mrs. Reinhold's purity of motive. What I have become skeptical about is the end result, the weakening of a human being's capacity to take care of himself, that appears to be inherent in protecting "unfortunates" from life's harsh blows. The act of helping, especially when helping is a professional commitment, carries a built-in high risk of doing subtle and profound harm to the intended beneficiaries (although it may do enormous psychological good for those who appoint themselves benefactors).

What well-meaning decision maker, no doubt with numerous advanced degrees in pedagogy and social work, decided that basket weaving is the salvation of the blind? The worst of the decision was not that it was stupid, but that the decision maker had the power to force it upon thousands of students, branding into their hides the contemptuous self-image of uselessness.

Sorry, Overbrook, I don't mean to single you out for attack after all the positive and wonderful things you did for me and others. My deep irritation is not with you, but with an attitude that permeates (with only a few islands of exception*) the blind establishment, in which you are only a speck.

Nobody who proves his competence in math and science should be reduced to enforced basket weaving when it's perfectly clear he or she is capable of being a computer programmer. And any reasonably alert blind person who lacks academic talent can do a broad range of manual work, including electronic assembly that might go into the manufacture of that computer. If my friend the administrator and basket-weaving enthusiast protests that, yes, our students can do those real-world tasks but real-world employers won't hire them to do it, my answer is he ought to direct his attention, his wit, and his power to educating those employers about the potential of blind people instead of educating blind kids to hate themselves.

Every year Overbrook, typical of other blind schools, has a Career Day. The kids have heard speeches by a blind congressman, a blind insurance salesman, a blind lawyer.

---

* The most notable exception in my experience is Recordings for the Blind, a national network of marvelous people, mostly volunteers, who perform the specific service of reading books onto tapes with skill and devotion. They have enriched my life and almost every blind person's by helping us become more independent.

Good speeches, good people, but no speeches that would encourage an ambitious kid to think he might possibly break new ground. I've never heard, at Overbrook and rarely anywhere else, a blind kid asked, "What are you interested in?" as a prelude to figuring out how that kid's ambition might be made feasible. Even if that ambition were not feasible, a counselor could use the information to guide the kid toward a more feasible career that would draw on the same interests.

I must get off my chest that I feel deeply hurt—for the sake of kids unknown to me who are now at Overbrook—that I have never been asked to speak at my own school's Career Day. The reason is perfectly clear, and has nothing to do with me personally. The reason is that professional educators of the blind fear encouraging the bright child to aspire. That's a strain of the same social disease—misguided compassion—that afflicted those teachers in ghetto schools.

Overbrook's failure to invite me to speak has not surprised me. Not only was I already familiar with the prevailing attitude at Overbrook, but I had also endured the attitudes of the blind establishment in my dealing with the Pennsylvania Bureau for the Visually Handicapped, which is typical of such bureaus in most other states. Again, I must apologize for being sharply critical of an agency that has helped me, but there are things that must be said.

During my early years of college, I had little reason to complain about the bureau. They sent the money, and that's all that I (or my school bursar) really wanted of them. Toward the end of my college years, however, when I said I wanted to apply to medical school and wanted their help in making contacts, and exploring the possibility of a career in medicine, they dropped me as though I had leprosy. I wrote and phoned and pressed, but could get no help.

When I approached the bureau about financial help, there

was lots of bureaucratic hemming and hawing: "There's no regulation covering medical school because no blind person has ever . . ."

After agonizing months of forcing my questions up to higher echelons of their bureaucracy, I finally got a top guy on the phone who heard me out, then said resolutely, "Well, there's a clause in the law that says we're supposed to support people through training schools. A medical school is a training school. If you get in, sure, we'll support you."

The state's Bureau for the Visually Handicapped kept giving me a hard time even after I was in medical school. I started at Temple in September, but weeks went by and the payment to the school and the subsistence stipend for me failed to arrive. The school understandably bugged me about it, and I had to bug the bureau. Finally one of their counselors came to see me in my dorm. He seemed suspicious, cold, unfriendly, and after some parrying I decided to break through his wall directly.

"You don't think I can do it, do you?" I said flatly.

"I'll be frank with you, I don't think you can."

He tossed out dribs and drabs of objections, all the tiresome, standard ones: How are you going to look into someone's eyes, a throat, see a rash, read a blood-pressure gauge, look into a microscope?

To keep from telling him off took all the control I had. I recited quietly that an eminent committee of doctors who passed on admissions to a leading medical school had already determined that for those simple matters a nurse's eyes were often as useful as the doctor's; that in any medical practice a doctor refers important observations like reading X rays, EKG's, performing special tests, to another doctor specializing in them; that a doctor's central function was to make diagnostic and treatment decisions based on medical data collected from a variety of sources, including nurses, lab tests, and specialists.

But I didn't tell him off. I needed the money. I just switched on a tone that I had learned to be good at, the conversational equivalent of patting his fanny and massaging it: "You're probably bringing up good points, but I think I have the right to try. And I think I can do it. And these doctors here think I can do it. And I feel that your agency should be working with me and rooting for me." Then I curved my reply around to embrace him a bit. "In the future, I hope to use my training to help blind people, the way you do. I hope you and I stay in contact because there's a lot I could learn from all the experience you've had."

For the first three years of my medical schooling, I had to fret all through each fall, calling the state persistently to get the money they'd committed to Temple and to me. Seldom did it come on time. Sometimes when I'd call, instead of excuses I'd get a shock. Some bureaucrat would say, "Well, it's been delayed because we have to relook at this."

"What do you mean 'relook'?" I'd demand. "It's been decided. It's been committed."

"Medical school costs an awful lot of money."

"It does for every medical student."

"Well, the costs have just gone up."

"The cost of everything has gone up."

By January they'd finally get around to paying it—when the bursar's office was at the end of its rope.

When nothing else broke their stalling, I'd remind some highly placed bureaucrat that the fundamental calling of his job and his department was to explore new vocations for blind people. I'm exploring one, I'd remind him. That always ended it, but I'd always hang up the phone with the detested feeling that he'd made me play the blind beggar.

I wish agencies for the blind would ponder the case of a man who lived near me. He's about 95 percent blind and, believe it or not, a carpenter. He must be a very good one because he apparently earns a good steady living and he has a nice home, which he fixes up himself. I couldn't imagine myself daring to become a carpenter.

Counselors and teachers of the blind don't have to start encouraging their aspiring clients and students to smash the stereotype by all becoming doctors or lawyers. They ought to seek out and publicize the great numbers of blind people who are succeeding in other skilled jobs, like auto mechanics and at least one poultry farmer I know of right here in Pennsylvania—named, incredible as it may seem, David Hartman!

Any blind person who becomes a carpenter or auto mechanic or poultry farmer is making the same point and, by my standards, his or her accomplishment is every bit as significant as my getting into medical school. What we have in common is that all of us have refused to accept the myth that blindness is necessarily more crippling than common handicaps with which people walk around all the time, holding good jobs—the handicap of a missing limb; of racial difference; of emotional hang-ups; of diabetes; of too many children to support; of coming from another country and having language and culture difficulties; of being afraid to drive a car; of feeling terrified at having to address strangers or groups. These are all serious life handicaps and career handicaps. *Everybody* in some way is seriously handicapped, but some handicaps, blindness among them, are more dramatic than others, more visible, and make it easier to class their possessors as total cripples.

The true pity of it is that no blind school or teacher or counselor ever gave my carpenter friend or me, or any other blind person I know, some realistic yet inspiring guidance about what to aspire to.

There is one more thing I want to get off my chest. I was vaguely, uncomfortably aware of this over many years of dealing with institutions for the blind, but the feeling came into focus during a portion of my medical residency that concentrated on physiatry, when I studied what's supposed to be done to rehabilitate patients who have just lost their sight. Experts informed us that a newly blinded person is headed for a spell of severe depression. The rule book says so. If the patient does not become depressed, he's a suppressor and a denier, and it's imperative, imply the experts, that you first cure the patient of that.

Clearly, if a patient has managed not to become severely depressed, and if his doctors insist he's got to be depressed or else there's something wrong with him, he's damn well going to be depressed by the time the experts are through. And if by some chance he still isn't, the experts will just declare him untrainable, owing to clear-cut maladjustment. I learned of an agency for the blind in Los Angeles that mapped it all out—literally. They prepared embossed pictures for newly blinded people to feel. The pictures express, through some sort of artistic symbolism, what the newly blinded person can expect—is *required*—to feel, starting with the immediate feeling of loss and going through predetermined phases until the final acceptance of blindness. They're practically telling these patients: If you feel something different than what we say, you're breaking the rules and there's something wrong with you.

That's what too many institutions wind up being all about. They start out of someone's desire to help individuals needing help. Then, for the sake of orderliness and efficiency, they start systematizing that help, creating general rules for all to follow, whether the rules are helpful to each individual or not. The person needing individual help is sternly informed that he must observe the rules, because that's the only way the institution can do its work. Before you know it, the needs of the institution, which by now is living a demanding life of its own, start taking priority over the needs of the individuals whom the institution is supposedly serving. It becomes the duty of the individual to bend his life to serve the institution's needs.

Take schools, where some troubled kids send up anguished signals that the institution is not serving their individual needs—the signals of vandalism, cutting classes, defying teachers by refusing to do classwork. When the signals become loud and clear enough, what is the school's answer? Suspension. If suspension doesn't work, expulsion. That's fine for the neat operation of the institution, but how about those kids? When Overbrook suspended Helaine for exchanging hot love letters with her Lothario, who was being protected and helped? Helaine or Overbrook?

My favorite recent example is one I encountered at a Canadian agency I visited to take part in a panel on education of the blind. An administrator told me of a transition-to-college program he had developed in which blind people come in for eight weeks to learn college study methods and how to take care of themselves. I was impressed. I wished I'd had something like that, especially some training in setting up a place to live, getting myself from residence to campus, and so forth. The protected life I lived in a college dorm, added to my upbringing in a small town, is responsible for my handicap to this day of not being able to move confidently around a city.

"Where do you put your people up?" I asked.

"Oh, they have to live here. We have a dorm."

"Everybody? Can they choose to live elsewhere?"

"No, we have to use that dorm."

"Why?"

"Because the dorm was built for that purpose and involved a heavy investment. So, financially, it's important for the program to have them stay here."

I know of one educator of the blind who refuses to accept the sneak-play reversal of making people serve institutions that were originally organized to serve people. The person I have in mind, although I'm sure there are others, is Dr. Nancy Bryant, who heads the Michigan School for the Blind. Dr. Bryant, in a sense, is devoted to doing away with her own job and her institution, or at least vastly changing them. She is determined to move as many of her students as possible out of the Michigan School for the Blind and into public schools.

I wish Overbrook had encouraged and prepared me to leave as soon as I could, instead of making me feel guilty about leaving. I wish they had encouraged other academically able students, those best able to make it on the outside, to leave, instead of fighting tooth-and-nail to keep us. No matter how you slice it, they were suppressing the individual for the sake of the institution. To survive, institutions must suppress individuals.

Integration of blind students with sighted students accomplishes many things at one blow. For the blind student who's ready for it, integration is the best training for life in the real world. It also teaches sighted people what blind people are like, what they can and can't do, and how to relax with blind people as with anyone else. Thirdly, increased integration would put pressure on teachers in public schools to learn the few adjustments necessary to accommodate special needs of blind students.

Schools for the blind, Dr. Bryant has come to believe, must increasingly devote themselves to blind students of such severe multiple handicap—blindness and mental retardation, blindness and deafness—that they can't handle instruction in a public school. But children with other kinds of multiple handicap, such as blindness and lameness, might be encouraged, with some special assistance, to study in classes of the sighted to live in a world of the sighted.

That, in perhaps too simple summary, is what Nancy Bryant believes. And I agree with her.

Maybe I should add, so you'll know where my prejudices partly come from, that I further admire Dr. Bryant for having the good taste to invite me to speak to her students. I talk at colleges and blind-establishment banquets and for do-good groups of various kinds, always being exhibited as Mr. Exception, the Blind Wonder Boy. But only two schools for blind youngsters—Michigan's and another on the island of Jamaica—have permitted me to upset their kids with the idea that they need not be useless and hopeless and beggars and basket weavers, that they ought to reach out and try to find their true limits. Nancy Bryant is not afraid to let a blind doctor stand up in her school assembly and say, "Maybe you can be what you want to be, too."

16

And Now the Story Begins

I have devoted many of these pages to convincing you—and devoted much of my life to convincing my family, my schoolteachers, my college professors, and numerous admissions committees of medical schools—that I want to be a psychiatrist, nothing but a psychiatrist, and that I won't happily settle for anything else.

That's not exactly true. Another vision of myself has nagged at me ever since my earliest days of adoring Uncle Chill; it persisted all during my science studies in school and college, and often flashed across my mind during my years at Temple, and especially during nights on duty in the hospital emergency room. Part of me really wants to be the all-around, night-riding, black-bag-toting family doctor, the kind known to all through old movies and modern television. When his telephone rings, he's off into the streets to save a life. In a race to the emergency room, he arrives in a photo finish with his patient, tearing off his coat, rolling up his sleeves, pumping on that chest, calling, "Shoot the atropine. Give this. Give that. Okay, now we're going to move him—up and easy." He's the center of the action, in command of it. Even the patient is only a supporting player.

That's my fantasy. Always has been.

Needless to say, that Hollywood fantasy could not survive the clinical experience that I—or any doctor—went through in the opening years of hospital internship and residency. The particular lesson for me was that I didn't really want to be a family doctor, even if I could be one. At least I knew I wouldn't like it for long. A great deal of a general medical practice deals with the frustrations of colds, strep throats, urinary infections, pneumonia, and other such diseases. Treating these diseases holds no particular appeal for me.

I write these closing pages two years, almost to the day, after receiving my medical degree. These two years have been a treasure of practical doctoring experience. The first year of my hospital residency, which used to be called the year of internship, I spent at Temple's hospital preparing to specialize in rehabilitative medicine. That's a relatively new specialty with a new name, physiatry. I was seriously considering going for a double career specialty of psychiatry and physiatry. Physiatry deals with patients who have experienced physical trauma. They are victims of strokes, disabling and disfiguring accidents, amputations, paralysis resulting from a damaged or severed spinal cord. These people have to learn a new style of physical life and, consequently, must redesign their psychological lives. That's right down my alley. I've had to do it—shaping attitudes to the realities of my physical limitations—every day of my life. So I start out perhaps better equipped to help these people than most doctors.

During my hospital year in physiatry, when a patient told me of his or her arthritic ache, I'd examine the elbow, or the knee, or the knuckles, give an injection, and feel better at the patient feeling better. But what really fascinated me was talking to the patient—to the person: finding out what kind of work he does, whether he's married, whether she has children, whether he's lonely, whether she has hobbies, how the illness that brought him here fits in with the rest of his life.

And being a doctor, a trained medical person, has helped, just as being blind has helped. When a woman tells me, "I've had three abortions," I know something of the physical as well as psychological implications of what she's saying. I've performed abortions. I comprehend their bodily as well as emotional effects. When a patient's chart says she has muscular dystrophy, it's very important for the doctor, the psychological doctor, to understand what muscular dystrophy is.

During the past year, the second year of my residency, I have served in the psychiatric department of the University of Pennsylvania Hospital. It has been the most fulfilling and secure year of my life. The work, the role, the life of being a psychiatrist feel right, feel fruitful. The doubts and doubters I have always had to contend with, those endlessly repetitive demands to keep proving and proving and proving, are largely gone.

I am a doctor here. I feel like a doctor. I feel accepted as a doctor. I know I've come to the right place.